Dog Training 101
The Book That Puts You In Control

Karen Duet

Copyright © 2007 Karen Duet
All rights reserved.

ISBN: 1-4196-6892-7
ISBN-13: 978-1419668920

Visit www.booksurge.com to order additional copies.

PREFACE		1
I.	What am I getting myself into?	5
II.	Choosing your Dog	23
III.	The Concept of Confinement Conditioning	45
IV.	Dog Behavior and Psychology	71
V.	Puppy Pre-School (2-4 months)	105
VI.	Elementary School - Basic Obedience (4-8 months)	129
VII.	Problem Solving & Manners	163
VIII.	Middle School – Off Leash Obedience (9-12 months)	197
IX.	High School - Advanced Obedience and Agilities (12-18 months)	213
X.	Dealing with Dominance and Aggression Issues	233
XI.	Traveling with Your Canine Companion	303
XII.	College for Dogs (Titles and Certifications)	315
About the Author		339
A Letter From the Author		343
Glossary of Terms		345
Suggested Reading		371

PREFACE

Most people who decide to add a new dog to their lives picture a perfect scenario. This usually entails visions of sunny afternoons spent with the dog playing with the children, long comfortable walks in the park and a calm pet lying by the fireplace while the owners read or watch television in peace. While these more sublime visions might emerge after time and hard work, they will not happen automatically; much like when a couple decides to have a child, they usually don't focus on the diaper changing and sleepless nights. Dogs are not born with remote controls, but they certainly are born with minds of their own. Getting a dog to this imagined point of perfection takes time, consistency, training, and patience.

The dream dog and the untarnished furniture that comes with it will require a plan. By the time you've finished this book, you will have that plan. The proper strategy should include easy-to-follow instructions along the way, which allows you to periodically judge how you are doing and how far you have to go to arrive at the finish line.

Your dog can be one of the biggest joys in your life, or he can be the cause of heartache. Some people look at this fact as the luck of the draw, but the truth is that a great deal can be done to affect the outcome.

There has been much argument over the years with regard to whether nature or nurture is more important in shaping your dog's personality. While both are certainly important, the experiences of nearly three decades of training dogs lead us to conclude that the breakdown is roughly 60 percent nature and 40 percent nurture.

Thus, while a well bred puppy may be put in a less than desirable environment, he may well be rehabilitated successfully because of his genetic propensity for stability. A genetically instable temperament, by contrast, would not be able to be rehabilitated past the level predetermined by his genetics. A prime example of this principle is a poor nervous system, the best indication of which is how quickly and dramatically a dog responds to stimulus. These traits will not change, regardless of environment.

We have all heard stories about great dogs that have positively affected the lives of the people who love them. But while we have seen the television movie heroes such as Lassie and Rin Tin Tin, we have also seen Pit Bull attacks on the evening news. We know of people whose dogs have lived long and healthy lives, and we also know of people who have had devastating veterinary bills and lost their dogs early to illnesses.

The question then becomes what you can do to stack the odds in favor of your success? Although there is no way to have a 100 percent guarantee, there are some guidelines that you can follow in order to steer toward success. The purpose of this book is to allow you to create such a plan. It is written based upon a system that has been tested on literally thousands of households and dogs for over a quarter of a century.

Last but not least, a word about the tactics we use to get you to your final goal. After years of experience with owners and their dogs, we have seen one theme repeat itself over and over again, when owners finally throw up their hands in frustration and declare that the dog must be trained or he has to go. That theme is one of spoiling and lack of supervision. The effects of spoiling and lack of supervision build up over months and often explode in an event that is the catalyst for seeking a training course. This catalyst may be the destruction of a valuable possession or aggression toward a family member.

Much like human children (who's education this book parallels), dogs need structure, boundaries on their behavior, and supervision in order to thrive and to keep them from being hurt or hurting others. In this way some of the underlying themes in this book could be applied to raising children by giving them the aforementioned boundaries for their behavior and teaching them to earn their freedoms by establishing proper behavior patterns. Although the way that parents go about this process is different with children than with dogs, it is our hope that the reader will also grasp the underlying methods and psychology in this work. We wish you the best training experience you can have with your canine companion!

Is this what you picture happening to your home when you think of owning a dog?

I. WHAT AM I GETTING MYSELF INTO?

When you make the decision to bring a new dog into your home, it is important that you fully understand all of the responsibilities and potential difficulties that go with this decision. The new dog is probably going to be with you, day in and day out, for the next decade. This is a decision that must not be entered into lightly. A puppy is not a toy that can be discarded easily when it is no longer cute or convenient. Often times children's emotional attachments are involved and careful thought should be given to this fact before a puppy or dog is purchased on a whim. Adult emotions, however, are equally important. Many problems have been caused to marriages by one party who welcomes the new dog and the spouse who cannot be bothered with the responsibility.

Choosing an older dog from a shelter or a rescue can also present challenges. Previously-owned dogs can come with baggage that you will not be aware of until you live with the dog for awhile. Destructive habits, running away, shyness or aggression due to abuse, and housebreaking issues are just a few of the things that you might find yourself dealing with simply because someone else didn't bother to train the dog properly.

Because of the commitment you are making when purchasing a new dog or puppy, you should always look at the various costs to your family (both in time and money) that this commitment will demand and determine whether or not you are willing to take on this additional responsibility. Keep in mind that the costs of a dog will be the same whether you choose to start out with a purebred from a breeder or an adopted dog from the shelter. The only difference in actual cost will be the purchase price. After this initial investment, the costs in both time and money will essentially be the same other than any illnesses or genetic maladies that might be present at your purchase.

COSTS:
Veterinary Care

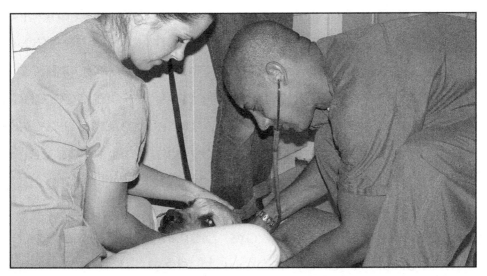

A veterinarian that you can trust is essential to owning a dog.

You will immediately want to schedule a veterinary appointment for your new dog or puppy. You will want him to have a physical examination to make sure that your new pet is in good health and is free of parasites. You will also want to get on a shot program with your veterinarian, as well as discuss other issues such as flea and parasite control. It is highly recommended that you have an identification microchip inserted into the nape of your dog's neck so that he could be tracked back to your address and phone number if he were to get lost. This simple step will prevent your pet from ending up in a shelter or even being euthanized if he gets lost. You and your veterinarian will also need to discuss the proper nutritional needs for the age and breed of your dog and make sure that his diet stays consistent, both in regard to content and feeding times. You should be aware that feeding a dog properly may often cost more than the price of simple grocery store dog food, but it can pay off in both the health of your dog and in less visits to the veterinarian. There are also several supplements on the market for skin and coat care that might be necessary or helpful depending on the breed of dog and coat type. If you are going to own a dog, you should always plan to have enough discretionary money in your budget to react to a medical emergency. Remember that dogs (like children) often find ways to injure themselves. If this is an issue that scares you, you might consider purchasing health care insurance for your dog.

Grooming

Grooming a dog can be simple or complicated, depending on the type of dog that you purchase. Long-coated breeds will require regular brushing and professional grooming on an average of once per month. Grooming can get expensive, in addition to eating up the time taken to transport the dog back and forth. If you try to groom a long coated breed yourself, you must consult a professional groomer for advice. Many owners make the mistake of trying to groom their own dogs and then end up brushing only the outer coat of the dog. This causes mats in the dog's coat that can be very painful and even tear the skin open. Groomers can tell you horror sto-

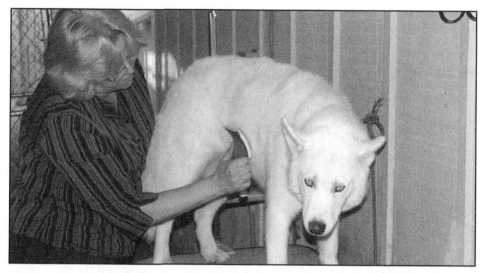

A groomer as part of your team of professionals will help you maintain your dogs cleanliness and health.

ries about what they have seen when novice owners attempt to groom their own dogs. At the very least, the dog may have to be shaved down in order to let the hair grow out again. At worst, it will cost you veterinary bills because of infected ears, impacted anal glands, mats that have torn the skin, and infections. If you purchase a "wash and wear" dog with a short coat such as a Boxer or Labrador, grooming will be much easier for you to do on your own, but it is still wise to have a professional groomer care for your dog on a quarterly basis between the baths that you provide. This allows for cleaning of the ears and anal glands, which you may have missed, as well as toenail trimming. It also enables you to ask any questions related to the dog's skin and coat condition.

Housing and Equipment

Everybody knows that if you get a bird you will need a bird cage. A fish requires a fish bowl; a horse requires a stall, etc. So why is it that people think that a dog can freely roam around their house when he first comes home without getting in trouble?

Properly training your dog to live in your house takes time and effort. Until the day that he earns his freedom, you will need containment areas in the form of a dog run (or a puppy pen if you own a young dog) and a crate, as well as proper feeding pans and water bowl and toys. For your dog's waste, a pooper scooper is recommended, along with a sealed, lined trash can with an airtight lid. If used correctly, this can be sealed and put out with your trash for pick up.

TRAINING

Locating a professional trainer to help you through your dogs formative years will go a long way to easing your stress and adding to your enjoyment of the dog.

One thing you should never overlook is the importance of training for creating a positive atmosphere for you and your new dog. There are many questions that arise as to how to best housebreak, stop behavior problems, and teach obedience, often leading to heated arguments about the most appropriate way to train a new dog. The easiest solution is to hire a professional trainer, who will guide you through the few months where the problems can be most easily dealt with.

There are many different training options and styles to choose from, though they will vary depending on where you live. Among your foremost considerations in choosing a trainer should be avoiding abusive programs. Physical abuse in the form of kicking, hitting, hanging or shocking a dog is always unacceptable. The only valid reason for a trainer to hold a dog off the ground is in defense of themselves when the dog is trying to bite them or someone else. Except for cases of self-defense, you should never see anything but encouragement, reward, and corrections that are mild enough to be clear to the dog without squelching his spirit. This is the delicate line that a good trainer walks. It is similar to parenting skills insofar as you need to let the dog know that you are serious, while at the same time letting him know that as soon as he accomplishes the task that you have asked of him he will receive the praise and reward that he seeks. In this way the dog learns how to acquire the behaviors that avoid correction or a lack of reward. This is basic strategy you should seek in your quest to find a good trainer.

Professional training takes: time (consistency and repetition), skill (knowledge of how to apply training to a variety of temperaments), and physical ability (in the beginning stages many dogs will jump on you, pull, bump your knees, etc). Types of training vary from location to location; however, you will usually find four different ways that training is offered:

Group Classes: This is the least expensive way to do training, but it has many fundamental problems. Many owners have a hard time showing up consistently each week at the same time. Life happens and people get sick, they have commitments with their children, they go on vacation, etc. In a group class, you can't catch up once you fall behind. You are also expected to practice each week for 30–40 minutes per night. If a person falls behind on this responsibility, he or she is often embarrassed and may choose not to return. Another factor is difficult dogs. If your dog is overly distracted by a difficult dog in the class, neither of you may learn the lesson. If your dog is too difficult, he may be asked to leave or you might not find yourself in an environment where the instructor has enough time to deal with all of your dog's issues properly as an aggressive dog or excessively unruly dog generally demands more of the instructors time as opposed to a more passive and pliable dog.

One of the problems with group training is that there just isn't enough time for one instructor to deal with all of the owners' and dogs' personalities. Thus, these classes tend to heavily favor the dogs that are the easiest to work with from the get-go. The class environment may also work well for someone who has been through training before and just wants a structured environment in which to touch up their abilities. All of this will depend, of course, on the people that are in the class and the knowledge of the instructor. If you do choose to go this route, make sure that the instructor is a professional trainer or an obedience director for a dog club, etc. Do not make the mistake of going to a store where a cashier is christened as a dog trainer overnight and is running a class in order to sell merchandise. The price might be right, but the old adage that you get what you pay for will most likely be true.

Private On-Field Lessons: These are generally lessons that are given on a private basis at the trainer's location. This is different from group class training, as the trainer is exclusively yours for the hour. Private On-Field lessons are generally conducted at the trainer's facility. The advantage of this new location to your dog is the distractions that are provided since he is away from home. In some cases, other trainers may be present working with dogs, and this provides another distraction that can actually work as a benefit to your training. Another benefit of this type of one-on-one training is that most trainers will allow you to reschedule the lessons if you are sick or can't show up for some reason. The only difficulties presented by these lessons is that while obedience is accomplished, problem solving that revolves around the home (such as housebreaking, chewing, stealing things, etc.) can be discussed but not worked on, due to the fact that the trainer is never in the home. These lessons are generally two to four times more expensive than group classes but are also typically two to four times more effective in teaching the owner and dog together as a team. The owner is still expected to do homework 30–40 minutes per day, but normally the lessons can be postponed to a reasonable degree if the owner is out of town or cannot practice for another reason.

Private In-Home Training

This training goes one step further for the convenience of the owner. In this type of training, it is the trainer's responsibility to drive to the owner's home each week and give the lesson. Of course, the owner is going to pay more for this service. On average, the cost will be two to four times more expensive than the private on-field lessons, and the drawback is that some of your money will be used for the trainer's time and traveling expenses. On the upside, the trainer is going to see your home and be able to help you make decisions as to what to do about your dog's behavior problems.

Home manners such as stopping at doors and gates can be taught on location. Teaching the dog to go lie down in a specific place in the house can be practiced with the trainer there. Behavior problems, such as excessive barking when company arrives or chewing and stealing items, can all be worked on where they happen. Stopping at boundaries and not going in the street can be worked on at the scene of the crime rather than in an unrealistically sterile training environment. Having a private in-home trainer is akin to having a private trainer come to your house to get you into shape; it is a major convenience for the owner, and the dog is never out of its comfort zone. Therein lies the rub. The downside to this style of training for many is precisely that it is so convenient. Some dogs need to work around the distractions, or they will be perfectly behaved at home and then act like monsters when they go out in public. In addition, some dogs are so territorial and spoiled in their own homes that the trainer cannot get enough control over the dog in each session to get anything accomplished. The owners also can be a problem. People who desire the convenience of the in-home lessons are often too busy to follow up with the training regime for 30–40 minutes per day. Since dogs learn by consistency and repetition, owners are essentially wasting their money by not following through. The follow up is out of the trainer's control. Even the best trainer is heavily dependent on the effort that the owner is willing to put into the training process. We have had many clients in our in-home lessons, who cannot focus long enough to take the lesson due to ringing cell phones, screaming children, and the arrival of guests or family members. This training usually works well for people who are devoted to training the dog themselves and have the time to do so. This is the best training for someone who absolutely does not want their dog to go to a kennel and whose dog is already well-socialized and non-aggressive.

In-Kennel, In-Home Combination

This type of program is the Mercedes Benz of dog training. Because of this, it is also the most expensive, and you can plan to spend two to three times as much as you would for in-home lessons. This process involves the dog first being trained by the staff in the kennel. The owner does not have to do the daily training in this case because it is being done for them. The owner simply returns in the time allotted (which in our facility is generally 3–4 weeks) and at that point the owner is given a demonstration of what the dog has learned. The trainer then works with the owner and dog prior to releasing the dog to go home. This is followed by a lesson at the client's home and another follow-up lesson, typically on the trainer's field. Variations on the length of stay and the number of lessons can be made from program to program, but the course is always basically the same in that the dog is trained first, followed by the owner. The reason that this works so well is that the trainer does not have to rely on the owner to train the dog. The dog learns much faster because the trainer isn't making the mistakes that the owner would make in communicating key lessons to the dog. When the owner takes over, they are already very happy with the dog's progress and encouraged to try to get the dog to perform as well for them. When the trainer comes to the home, it solidifies in the dog's mind that the training is to be followed in more locations than just the kennel. This also gives the trainer the opportunity to establish in-home manners such as not running through open doors, staying within boundaries, and the place command, as well as problem solving. It is never recommended that you send a dog to a kennel for training and then take him home without a demonstration and at least 3 lessons with the dog and the trainer. The addition of the in-home lesson is invaluable in this situation because of what it means to the dog and owner to complete their education in their living space.

Time

You should ask yourself the question: "Do I have enough time to properly raise a puppy or add a dog to my life?" The process of raising a puppy is not much different from having a new baby in the house. Luckily, the qualifier is that this process takes months rather than years. Early puppy-raising involves getting up in the middle of the night to let the puppy out for a potty break and to stretch his little legs. There are fear (age of 8–12 weeks) and critical socialization periods (age of 6–16 weeks), where you need to give special attention to the puppy so that it grows up confident and well-socialized. The last thing you want to do is to leave the puppy home alone during this period to fend for itself. If you do leave him alone, the result will be a very difficult dog to train with little understanding of what you want from it as an adult. A puppy between 8-16 weeks old needs to be introduced to children and any other animals it is expected to live with. This has to be done in a way that does not scare or intimidate the puppy.

If you purchase an adult dog or puppy over four months of age, you can go directly into a training program. This will require a few weeks where you must be dedicated to 30–40 minutes of daily homework with the dog. The exception to this rule is if you take in-kennel training. Even with someone else doing the hardest part of the work for you, you must still practice for at least 20 minutes per day for 2–3 weeks afterwards. After this point, regardless of the training program, you will need to spend time to keep the training up. Your best results will come from weaving the training and rules you have set for your dog into your daily routine. It is a good idea to take your dog on a daily walk, where you practice all of your obedience commands, keeping up on the rules that you have established like stopping at doors and gates, and using the place command. The owner who spends the most time with the dog will have the best results. This is assuming that the time spent is balanced with all the aspects of praise, discipline, and fun (which should not be confused with spoiling). Though these time commitments may seem daunting, you would be surprised how often people with hectic work and parenting schedules still work a dog into the mix successfully. These people usually do so by having a plan and sticking with it. This may mean the use of professionals to help them get through the most difficult times, delegating tasks between family members, or sometimes simply waiting for the appropriate time to add a new member to the family.

Many people figure that they will have to tolerate having their possessions destroyed as part of having a new puppy or adult dog. They are generally sure that they will have to have housebreaking issues and tolerate the bad behavior that they expect from the puppy until the puppy "grows out of it." In writing this book, it is our intention to impart solutions that will help you through the rough patches. Although we cannot promise you that you will NEVER have to deal with a destroyed possession or a mess in the house, we can promise that if you follow the instruction in this book you will have far fewer accidents or tales of destruction to deal with.

Choosing to purchase a puppy or an adult dog is a big decision that shouldn't be taken lightly.

II. CHOOSING YOUR DOG OR PUPPY

Too many people when selecting a puppy or new dog are driven by impulse. They may purchase a puppy when visiting a pet store, or purchase a puppy in front of a grocery store. Not enough thought has gone into any of these decisions given that they are decisions made on a whim. Because this dog is hopefully going to spend the next decade with you it makes sense to put a good deal of thought and effort into the breed and temperament of the dog you purchase. This will be your companion and friend, and you will want to have the best shot possible at success both in temperament and in health. Be aware that different breeds of dogs have vastly different temperaments. You need to define what "your type" is prior to choosing. "Type" has to do with both physical attractiveness to you (this is different with everyone) and temperament. For instance, some people like the look of the wolf. In some cases these people are attracted to the Siberian Husky or the Alaskan Malamute. If they purchase one of these breeds on looks only, they may be dismayed to find out that these breeds do not train up as easily as the German Shepherd Dog even though the look is similar. Also, someone might purchase one of these Nordic Breeds for protection and be dismayed to find that they are typically more shy and reclusive like the wolf. It is for this reason that it is so important to understand what a breed was bred to do work-wise prior to your selection. Some people are taken with a breed because they have seen it in a movie or television show and thought that the dog depicted was cute or clever. They may assume that this is a true representation of the breed. In most cases this couldn't be further from the truth. When the Disney movie 101 Dalmatians was released, we had a dozen Dalmatians in our kennel within 6 months after the opening. Three of them were named "Pongo." The owners had all purchased the breed because their children had been taken with the movie. None of the new owners had a clue that this breed is very high strung and oftentimes deaf. The best advice we can offer a prospective owner is to do your research well ahead of time. Do not buy on a whim, but rather think out the decision well. How do you do this? Purchase books from the bookstore or library. There are several interactive computer programs that match you up with the best breed for you. AKC.Org is the American Kennel Club's website, and they offer a wealth of information on breeds, breed clubs, and breeder classified ads. You should ask yourself the following questions prior to making a choice: What type of breed do I find physically attractive? Small dogs, large dogs, large stocky Mastiff types, slender Grey Hound types, prick ears, cropped ears, flat ears, short coats, long coats, short round faces, long pointy faces? What activity level do you prefer? Do you bike ride and want a dog to jog next to you? Or are you a couch potato who would rather have a dog that wants nothing more than to curl up next to your couch and spend some time with you?

Do you have enough to do with your children that the last thing you need in your life is a high energy dog? Is your dog going to primarily live indoors or outdoors? You will need a breed that suits the environment you prefer. Certain breeds like Boxers, Dobermans, and Boston Terriers to name a few, have very little coat and do not do well kept outside. You should know whether a breed has a problem with extreme temperatures before you purchase. What level of trainability do you desire? If you have always had Hounds or Terriers and you find that they fit your needs and personality, then if it isn't broken, we won't worry about fixing it. On the other hand, if you desire to choose an easily trained dog, you should look at the Herding, Sporting, and some of the Working breeds, because these breeds were bred to work for and with man. They are easier to train than some other breeds that were bred to work independently or with packs of

Shown (L-R) German Shepherd (Herding) Labrador Retriever (Sporting) Bull mastiff (Working) All dogs in groups that were bred to work with humans which makes them more easily trainable than some of the other breeds that were not bred to work with humans.

dogs, such as Terriers and sled pulling breeds. Shepherds, for instance, were bred to take direction from the handler and use a great deal of intelligence in running livestock. The Border Collie and Belgian Shepherd for instance have always scored the highest in the K-9 IQ Tests. Of course, trainability has to be defined by the task at hand. If you are looking for a dog to go to ground after vermin or chase a fox, then Terriers and Hounds would naturally be your choice. What we are referring to here is the level of trainability suitable for your everyday dog that is going to learn obedience and perhaps travel on vacations with the owner.

How protective do you want the dog to be? Only a small percentage of dogs are suitable as real viable trained protection dogs. Some breeds will bark and make a lot of noise, but when push comes to shove, they will back down. If you are looking for a dog who will realistically protect you or can be trained to do so on command, you are narrowing your field to the Working and Herding categories and only some of those breeds will do the job. Breeds such as the German Shepherd, Belgian Shepherd, Belgian Malinois, Boxer, Bouvier, Bull Mastiff, Rottweiler, Pit Bull, and Doberman, to name a few on the short list, will do. It is very important to properly socialize and train these breeds so that they can also be good canine citizens while offering you extra protection. How friendly do you want your dog to be with other dogs and strangers? Various breeds are not at all alike. Gun dogs such as Retrievers and Spaniels have a good reputation for getting along because they have been bred to work around other dogs and people. This is similar for Hounds who hunt in packs, whereas Terriers are infamous for fighting with each other.

How much grooming do you want to be responsible for? Many long coated breeds will need a monthly grooming appointment to keep the coat from matting. People deceive themselves by thinking that they can keep up with the grooming themselves but often only groom the top coat of many layers. The result is a matted dog that is often in pain because of the hair being pulled tight against the skin. This often results in the actual tearing of the skin and causes pain and infection. The only way to prevent this is to keep up with the grooming properly or shave the coat down to a reasonable length. These are all things that you should ask yourself prior to making your choice. In this way you will be less likely to purchase a dog that is the wrong choice for your life. Once you are sure that you have selected the right breed for you, it is time to look at your options:

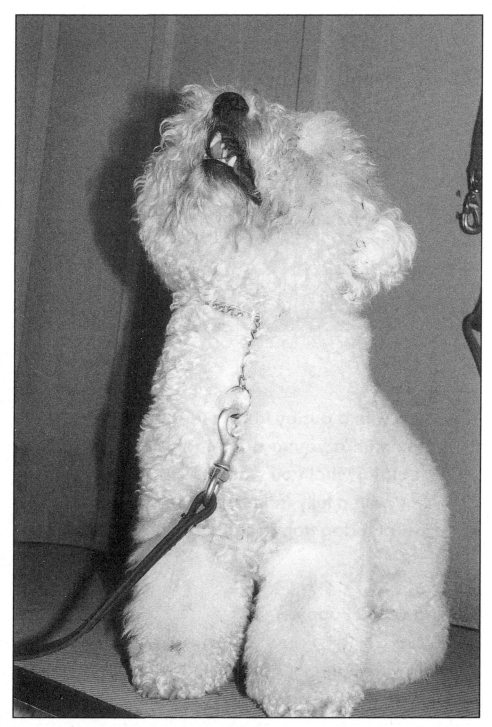
This Bichon Frise in need of grooming is an example of what you can face with a breed that requires regular coat care.

The same Bichon Frise after grooming

1. **Start with a puppy from a reputable breeder.**
2. **Start with a young adult that shows good prospects for what you want.**
3. **Start with a fully trained adult.**
4. **Adopt a dog from a shelter or breed rescue.**

Starting with a Puppy

If you are going to purchase a puppy, you will want to start by researching breeders. Not all breeders are created equal. A good breeder is one who has a definite idea of the purpose that they are breeding for, and it is always to better the breed. The breeder should have a standard for conformation and temperament. The breeder should have a history with the breed of producing quality dogs. You should be able to ask for references from past puppy buyers, and if the breeder has been in the breed for long enough, you should be able to confirm that their pups have attained titles or awards in something. The options could be Championships in conformation, obedience titles in the show ring, sport titles, tracking, agility, hunting, coursing, etc. In other words the breeder should have a purpose in mind for the pups. A common practice is for the top picks of the litter to go to those people who will be showing or sporting with the pups, and the rest of the pups may be sold as pets. This leaves several pups that may be perfect as pets but may lack the overall drives or conformation for the task the breeder has bred for. The breeder should be involved with a code of ethics club or at least have a contract that covers the typical maladies that the breed has a tendency toward and proof that the parents have been checked for these maladies. During the research you have done on this breed you should have come across the common health problems with the breed and be prepared to ask the breeder about the parents' health status with regard to these maladies. Do not purchase a puppy from a pet store or puppy mill. These types of operations are all about the money and tend to look at the puppies as a commodity that can be bought and sold. Typically these puppies are marked up at least 100%, and the thought that goes into their breeding is slim to none.

Authenticity of papers on these puppies is questionable, and often puppies that are from mixed breeding are represented as purebreds. In addition, these puppies tend to be in ill health and have been kept in living conditions that are small cramped spaces where they have had to eat, sleep, and eliminate in the same area. This situation makes housebreaking these puppies a nightmare. It is not unusual for buyers to find that the pups they purchased from establishments like these have compromised immune systems and ongoing difficulties such as hip and elbow dysplasia. What you want to see in a breeding facility is a nice warm environment for the bitch to whelp and the puppies to grow up in.

Puppies cannot regulate their body temperatures properly, so this is critical to their early health. Because of this, whelping the bitch indoors is critical. A laundry room or a basement with space heaters make good selections. An area near washing machines or dryers is ideal for changing the bedding, and these appliances create extra heat in the room. If it is summer time, air-conditioning vents should be shut off in the puppies' room. Whelping areas should be warm (not hot) and easy to clean. Leaving a door open is not a good idea because of drafts and flies. An ideal area is one where a doggy door can go into a dog run area so that the bitch can go in and out, and the puppies can do so as well later. Our set up features a doggy door from the tiled laundry room, where the bitch whelps that leads into an enclosed garage which has been converted into a room with a sliding glass door (providing light) and screen as well as a air-conditioner for summer use. This allows light and prevents flies. We have a puppy pen inside this area, where the puppies and mother come into the enclosure, and the area itself is covered in pine shavings. These shavings are eventually pushed back into half of the area when the puppies are weaned so that they may eat in the area not covered with shavings. In this way the puppies are housebroken very easily when they go to their new homes because they have learned to look for the area that smells like shavings to potty. This transfers easily to the home, where the owners can put shavings down in the area where they wish the puppy to potty. It doesn't take very long at all to condition the puppy to go to this area, and then the shavings are no longer necessary. When the puppies are old enough to begin to try to escape the whelping box, you simply close the doggy door off and use a crate instead of a whelping box for sleeping (take off the door from the crate) and put in a blanket so that the pups learn to sleep on the blanket and potty on the shavings. This should happen easily if the prior conditioning has already been accomplished and the area is large enough.

Puppies are very messy after they start eating solid food. At this point typically their mother refuses to clean up after them any longer. This is where the breeder has the difficult job of keeping the living quarters clean enough that the puppies do not walk in their own feces nor do they start eating them. This can become a filthy habit later on. Shavings help in this situation because the puppies will inadvertently kick shavings on top of the stool, and it will become buried. It is then less likely that the pups will eat the stool, and the shavings will keep the puppies cleaner. Even with this system, cleaning the shavings several times a day and replacing them completely every few days is necessary.

You should also see some type of a marking system so that the breeder can tell which puppies are gaining weight properly and can see easily which puppy has an illness or notice certain behavior traits more easily. A typical system is using yarn collars around the necks. This is not necessary if the coloring of the puppies' fur is very obviously different, or there are only a couple of puppies in the litter and differences are obvious. A good breeder should be able to tell you all about each pup's temperament and health history. This is one of the many drawbacks of buying a puppy from a pet store. There is nobody who can tell you the entire health and temperament history of the puppy and its siblings. A good breeder will also be there to answer questions for you in the future and to give you resources for local veterinarians, trainers, and groomers in your area.

Be aware that traditional crate training methods will not work or will be difficult to teach to puppies that have been raised in quarters that are too small or filthy. This is why it is very important for you to know where your puppy was raised and be happy with the conditions in which the breeder has raised the puppies.

A good breeder should not allow the puppies to go home to their new homes until they are at least 7 weeks of age. Typical ages to leave the breeders house will vary from breed to breed but should never be prior to 7 weeks. Prior to going home your puppy should have received at least one vaccination and should have been wormed at least twice. There may have been other medications given due to Cocidia, Giardia or other common conditions in puppies, and this information should be given to you as well so that you can be on the lookout for any reoccurrence of the same issues.

Your new puppy will have been started on a weaning formula and then put on a quality puppy diet. It is important that you keep the puppies diet consistent when it goes home, and any diet changes should be done slowly so as not to upset the puppies digestion system.

When purchasing a puppy, make sure that you meet both of the parents. The rule of thumb is not to expect your puppy to look better or have a better temperament than the parents. The seed doesn't usually fall far from the tree. There is usually no problem with viewing the mother because she is almost always owned by the breeder. In some cases you might have some difficulty in viewing the father due to distance or more recently the common use of frozen semen from deceased dogs or dogs from a great distance away. In this case you may need to do more research on what that dog was like and what offspring he has produced. The upside to this is that most people will not go to the trouble of using frozen semen unless they really believe the stud dog is worth reproducing.

Pros and Cons to purchasing a Puppy

The main drawback to purchasing a puppy is that there are no guarantees with regard to the outcome. You will not know for several months what kind of overall health and temperament the pup will develop in adulthood. Hip, elbow, and spinal problems can all be concerns. In some breeds blindness and deafness or heart problems can be concerns. The only insurance you can have against these issues is that the breeder did their best to test the parents for these issues and whether past litters have had the problems.

On the plus side of purchasing a puppy, you get to do all of the raising and imprinting. You don't acquire the baggage from something that someone else has done wrong with the puppy. If you expect your dog to function well with small children, or small animals or livestock, you can make sure that you socialize the pup well for these issues yourself. Also, if you have family members that are afraid of dogs, they will be much more likely to trust a dog they have known since it was a puppy.

Pros and Cons to purchasing a young adult

Some people wish to bypass the puppy stage as they may feel that they don't have the time to deal with the puppy. This often happens when people have small children and the thought of raising another baby is just too much.

Like any other option there are pros and cons to adopting a young dog between 6–18 months of age. On the upside you can see what type of temperament you are purchasing in the older pup. Around one year of age, you can have a complete health exam, including preliminary x-rays that will tell you whether there are any joint problems developing. At this age you won't have a final x-ray of hips and elbows, but you may be able to see a problem developing. This can save you some worries later on as well as expense.

On the other hand, dogs of this age tend to be teenagers and at their rowdy best! This is the age group where many dogs are given away due to jumping, digging and chewing problems and they are larger in size than they are mature. They are no longer in the cute puppy phase, but they are not at the calm mature stage either. Due to this set of circumstances this is a good time to hire a trainer to get involved right away. We have quite a few clients that will bring us their new young adult dog, prior to even taking it home. This can be helpful to start to train the dog what the rules of the house will be when he gets to his new home.

On the downside of purchasing the young green dog, you may have some baggage to deal with that other people have instilled along the way. This can be caused either by what they did or didn't do with the dog during the critical fear and socialization periods that happen between 2–4 months of age. The results of improper handling at this time in the puppy's life can be fear of strangers or other animals, fear of new situations, or overall fear and anxiety caused by abuse. In addition, if the dog was raised in a kennel situation with several other dogs and under-socialized with humans, the dog may have kennelosis and be completely incapable of dealing with humans while being very comfortable with other dogs. This is due to a lack of socialization with humans in the critical socialization period. This is common in large breeding kennels where the dogs are left alone for long periods of time and the only contact they have is with other dogs.

The success or failure you can have with this dog depends upon how much effort you are willing to put into rehabilitation. Of course, if your goals are more than creating a family pet, you should not start with a dog that is this far behind. A person that is looking to create an advanced dog such as a therapy canine, protection K-9, competition dog, etc., should always start with a well-socialized dog to begin with as these goals are hard enough to reach successfully without starting with a handicap.

Starting with a trained adult
Usually the reason that people start with an adult trained dog is one of two situations: The person doesn't feel he or she has the time to put into the raising or training of the dog that he or she wants, and he or she wishes to short cut all the way to the end result without the time and effort it takes otherwise.

The second reason is a person whose circumstances are such that they need the dog immediately. For instance, the person who has a stalker or has had an intruder may want a dog for protection immediately.

There should be caution used in this situation as there is a common knee jerk reaction when this happens, and sometimes the person will decide in just a few days that he or she really didn't need or want a dog after all. In other cases, adult dogs are purchased for the purpose of competition or service dog work simply because their aptitude for such work can be more easily evaluated at this age.

In the case of a protection dog, it is best not to choose to purchase an adult trained dog with children under school age unless you are absolutely sure that the dog has been socialized to children. The same goes for a situation where the dog must get along with other animals or livestock. You must be able to trust the agent that you will purchase the dog from so that you do not have a dangerous situation on your hands when you finally get the dog home. Many people are very happy with an adult trained dog, but just as many can tell you about nightmares where they paid several thousand dollars for a dog just to find out that it wanted to eat them alive when they picked it up from the airport or they discovered that the dog's papers or title had been falsified. Keep in mind that fully trained adult dogs are not inexpensive. They currently cost anywhere from $5,000.00–$10,000.00 depending on whether they are domestic or imported and whether or not they have a title. Highly titled breeding animals can cost much more than this. This might sound like a lot of money, but then on the other hand, 25% of this cost may be represented by the cost of a puppy of this quality and there are many hours of someone's time over a two to three year period that has gone into developing a fully trained dog. If you choose a fully trained dog you will always want to see a demonstration of the dog working and make sure that you have a trainer to work together with you and the dog after the purchase.

Purchasing sight unseen via the internet and phone calls is a bad idea. The pit falls here are mainly hidden health problems. At times people will sell a very nice dog who has a hidden health problem to unsuspecting buyers. It could be that the dog has parents that died early of cancer or a heart attack, and upon learning this the seller decided not to keep the dog due to this fact. There is no way for you or anyone else to be aware of this. This is especially true if the dog comes from another country. As with any other purchase, it is a "Buyer Beware" situation.

Adopting a dog from a Shelter or Breed Rescue
Adopting a dog from a shelter or breed rescue is an honorable thing to do. Many dogs that are abandoned

every day are fine dogs with nothing wrong with their health or temperament. Many of these dogs have done nothing wrong to end up in a shelter. Rather they found themselves in the middle of a divorce or a move, or some other human-originated situation that found them on the losing end. They are often the victims of negligence or abuse and sometimes the most trivial of human behavior such as giving a puppy to someone as a gift. Unless the person has chosen the puppy prior to the gift giving and has gone through the process of decision-making for this new addition with thought and consideration to everything previously mentioned in this book, there should never be a dog or puppy given as a gift. Everyone who has been involved with a shelter or rescue service can tell you that puppies given as gifts in a high percentage of cases will end up at a shelter or rescue when they are no longer cute little puppies. Because of this type of situation, there are breed rescues for every breed imaginable. You will find them easily on an internet search or by contacting your local breed club. A breed club is an excellent resource for you to learn more about a breed of dog and to find out what the typical concerns and health issues are for the breed. Dog shows are another place where you can go to view the breed you are interested in and inquire of the owners as to what the breed's pros and cons are. You can find a wealth of information about breeds and breed clubs and dog shows on AKC.Org. Many times, a rescue dog has had to learn to cope with the setting that he found himself in. It may have learned to jump fences in order to get food or water. It may have learned to jump on doors to get attention due to neglect or to dig or chew just to occupy his time. It may roll onto his back and cower or duck and run due to abuse. These issues can be handled but with some therapy so you will want to get the help of professional training as soon as possible.

Conclusion

Regardless of the age or origin of your choice in dogs it is critical that you deal with animal professionals who you can trust. This will take research on your part in order to find the right breeder, importer, veterinarian, trainer, and groomer who you will need to support your purchase and care of your new family member. Like so many other things in life, you will need to develop a routine care and maintenance program for your dog. After you locate your team of dog experts, life with the dog will be much easier because when you have a problem you can just pick up the phone and get advice from your team.

III. THE CONCEPT OF CONFINEMENT CONDITIONING

The Confinement Conditioning method does not make your dog a prisoner. You are ultimately in control of your dogs freedom. Proper behavior is rewarded with freedom.

WARNING!!!! DO NOT DISREGARD THIS CHAPTER AS IT IS THE KEY TO YOUR SUCCESS! We must start this chapter with a disclaimer: <u>We are not suggesting that you lock your dog up for the rest of his life!</u>

We are putting that statement right up front because for whatever reason with human psychology, humans tend to be all or nothing folks and have a hard time with a gradual system. In dog training, many things are a gradual progression and that is what many people fail to understand.

Dog Runs, Crates, Puppy Pens, and Baby Gates

The reason people tend to balk at these tools right out of the gate is that confinement to people represents negative concepts such as jail, solitary confinement, and zoos. When applied to your new dog or puppy, the concept should be more like a play pen, your child's bedroom, your child's crib, and car seat.

Dog Runs

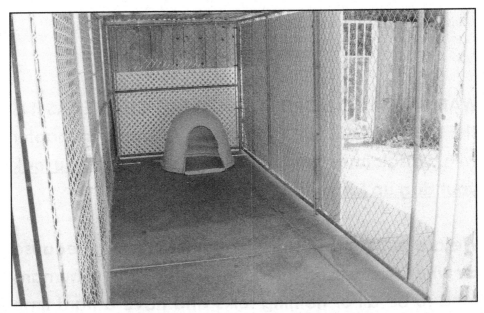

A basic minimum size dog run is 5 x 20 with solid fencing, cement or stone base, shelter from the elements, and cool clean water available at all times.

A dog run is a fenced area made specifically to hold a dog. This area should be a <u>minimum</u> of 5 foot wide by 20 foot long and 6 foot high. It can be used with or without a roof as long as there is shade available via a tree, canopy, or patio cover. The run can be larger, but should never be smaller than this. The fencing can be Wrought Iron or Chain Link as long as the following things are available for the comfort of the dog: fresh clean water available in a stainless steel bucket kept in the shade or an automatic watering system, shade (as mentioned above), shelter in the form of a dog house or other wind and rain resistant shelter, food at scheduled times, and toys for the dogs amusement. Think of this as the dog's bedroom where only his things should be. You should not have your trash cans or firewood, or anything else of yours in the dog run. The base of the run should be cement or cement pavers so that the dog cannot dig, will not be muddy if it rains, and so that it can be easily cleaned and washed down to create a fresh sanitary place for the dog to be kept. The most typical dog run is free standing chain link. It should be at least 11 gauge with reinforcing bars on the top, bottom, and in the middle. Thinner gauges and less reinforcement will just encourage the dog to try to break out by chewing or pulling at the fencing. From this most basic kennel set up you can go as wild as you want to. We had one celebrity client, who fenced a huge 30 x 60 area with Wrought Iron on cement for his Rottweiler. He then had a custom waterfall and pond put in one corner so that the dog could cool off if he wanted to. His dog house was a children's playhouse. Although this dog run represented a bit of Disneyland for dogs, it goes to show you how inventive you can be. The dog run is not to be confused with a "runner" or tie out for the dog. We do not believe in tying a dog out to anything when the owner is not right there next to the dog. The reason for this is that it is dangerous for the dog and others. The dog can injure itself by strangulation or wrapping the tie out line around his legs. It is a known fact that there is a high incidence of bites that occur when a dog is tied out or has a history of being tied out as it creates frustration.

What is the purpose of a Dog Run?
The ultimate purpose of the dog run is to teach the dog how to live in the yard without being destructive. Another use is to keep the dog safe from itself and others, and to keep others safe from your dog. Uses: you can leave for work knowing that your dog will be there and safe when you return. He will not have escaped the yard, been let out by gardeners or other workers, and will not be hit by a car or missing when

Some people get more elaborate with their dog runs. This one has wrought iron, lattice, and cement pavers as a base and is much larger than the 5 x 20 minimum.

you get home. You can leave home and know that when you get home you will not return to see that your possessions have been ruined or that you have large holes dug in your yard or worse. In addition, your dog will not be muddy or dirty from digging holes. You can clean up and power hose down and allow your children to play on the grass without stepping in dog feces. When the dog is put in the run at the times that you know he will need to go to the bathroom such as first thing in the morning and soon after eating, you will have very few stools to pick up in the yard. Cleaning cement is much easier to sanitize than the grass area. Your dog will be safe from falling in your pool, eating poisonous plants, and ingesting items that might cause him intestinal blockages. He will be safe from workers accidentally letting him out or him accidentally harming the workers. You can have invited quests over to your home without them having to wade through your dog/s in the process, which may cause them to be uncomfortable although they may be reluctant to express this to you for fear of you being insulted. You can separate younger dogs who need to learn how to live with freedom from older dogs who have earned their freedom. Your older dog will thank you for this. You can use the run to help prevent your dogs from breeding or being bred by other dogs you own or the neighborhood dogs, who may break into your yard in order to breed your female when she is in season. You can use your run to prevent your dog from jumping the fence (use a top on the run) if the dog has this habit or your fencing is not adequate to keep your dog in your yard.

Philosophy of the use of the Dog Run
First, we will explain again that we do not want your dog to spend its entire life in a dog run. For whatever reason many people have a hard time wrapping their minds around this concept. The concept (if applied correctly) will actually do the opposite. It will allow the

Essentials for owning a dog for cleanliness is a pooper scooper and a lined trash can for waste. The waste should be picked up at least daily and put out for removal weekly.

dog to live in freedom for the rest of his life. The idea is to <u>teach</u> the dog how to live properly in the house and yard without being destructive. Here is how it works: We all know that we cannot spend 24 hours per day watching our dogs. Most methods of problem solving will tell you to "catch him in the act." We know that we have a hard enough time watching our children every minute and between our children and our dog, we will choose to watch our children. A dog run allows you to put the dog back into a place that is "his" so that you can watch him when you have the time. A proper dog run allows him to meet all of his needs there. He can go to the bathroom, drink, exercise, play, and have shade and shelter. This is where he should eat and be given treats so that psychologically it is a positive place to be. Here is the key: You take the dog out of the run as many times per day *AS YOU CAN WATCH HIM AND ARE WILLING TO MONITOR HIS BEHAVIOR*. The younger he is the less the amount of time per session. Puppies may be out for only 10 minutes at a time several times per day. As the pup ages you can figure out just how long the pup can be out without getting in trouble. You gradually work your way up from 10 minutes to 15, 20, 25, 30, and so on. When the pup makes a mistake you must be there to create a negative association. This will be a negative taste, smell, or sound association. This will be discussed further in the next chapter. Learning to earn freedom is very important as habits are easily formed with a dog. Humans have a tendency to have a hard time with the idea of confinement since as children we are told "go to your room" if we are bad. If we do something really wrong, we are sent to jail. It is therefore a human reaction to think that the dog will think of things in the same way. We forget that the dog does not have any reasoning ability and does not have the same associations that we have. If a dog is raised using a dog run, you will actually see him asking to go back in when he is tired, hungry, or thirsty. That is because he is CONDITIONED to be comfortable in the run. This should be a SAFE PLACE for him if it is taught correctly.

Crates

Crates can be utilized from the very beginning with puppies. Most puppies cannot make it through the night in a crate until they are over 4 months old. If you are going to utilize a crate prior to this, you will have to be prepared to get up in the middle of the night. The crate should be looked at as the dog's bed. Much like a child's crib, this is where you can put a dog or puppy and walk away knowing that they are safe from harm. The crate is an excellent tool for the pup to learn that he has a bed that can be moved from

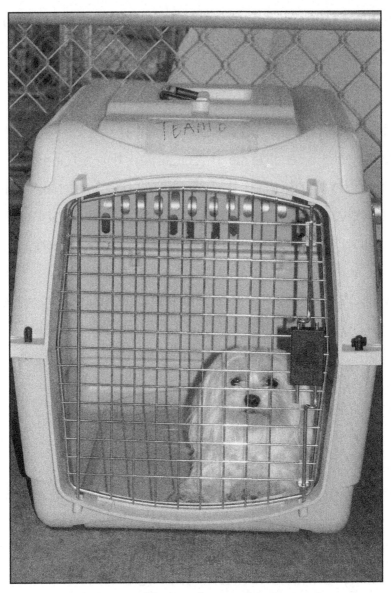

Crates should be used for confinement indoors where the dog can be kept comfortable in the air conditioned and heated home. The crate is also useful for safe transportation of the dog.

place to place. Another use for the crate is as a traveling car seat for the pup. If you use it to contain your dog in your vehicle, he won't be a projectile in your car should you be involved in an accident. Although there are specific uses for a wire crate, the best type for travel safety is the plastic enclosed type of crate. This type is safer in an accident and if the dog should vomit or have an accident in the crate this type will be much easier to clean and to keep the mess within it. It also makes the dog feel more secure as it is covered both on top and on the sides. You will find that there is much less hair and dirt in your car when you travel with the dog in a crate.

The crate should never be used to hold the dog 12–24 hours per day. The use of the crate should be strictly when the dog sleeps and for short periods through the day. If the dog is housed in the crate to sleep at night, it should be out in the run or under supervision for all but 4 more hours maximum during the day. This is because the dog needs a reasonable amount of time to stretch his legs, relieve himself, and explore its environment. If the weather does not permit the dog to be out in the run during the day, you should attempt to have a puppy pen set up in a basement, garage, or laundry room, where the dog can go in the crate to sleep but where the door is open so that the dog can come out and stretch and drink or potty. This area should have shavings in it if it is to be used for any long period of time such as during a cold snap or storm.

DOGGY DOORS USED IN CONJUNCTION WITH CRATES

This outside area for small dogs is protected from preditors by overhead cover and snake proof fencing that also prevents rodents from entering the home.

A doggy door used in conjunction with crates, in our opinion, is the best way to potty train medium to small breed dogs. It is easy on everyone, and it basically forces the dog to set a pattern of going to the bathroom outside. The only difficulty doing this with large dogs is the size of the doggy door. To create a doggy door for a large dog means a very large potential hole in the side of your house. This may well be large enough for an intruder to come in. These are all things you have to consider when deciding which method to use. Typically a medium or small

These small dogs are contained within the home in a wire crate attached to the wall. They can enter the doggy door and stay in the air-conditioned and heated home while not having the run of the house unless the door on the front of the crate is opened.

doggy door will not present that problem. There are also electronic doggy doors that will not allow the door to open unless the dog is near. The dog wears a collar that signals the door when he is near and the door latch opens. Doggy doors can be put in anything: Screen doors, walls, French doors, metal doors, you name it. Here in Southern California a couple of people have even made installing doggy doors into a business.

Most people who own small dogs want them indoors most of the time. The problem for them in accomplishing this is that they have to use the bathroom often, and it can be a full time job just trying to keep up with their schedule. This problem is solved by installing a doggy door in a convenient area of the home. Ours for instance is in a guest room that leads out to a back patio. It is important for this crate to be wire because the wire crates allow you to remove the back and attach the crate to the wall where the doggy door is. You want this crate to be very roomy because it will be where the dog can sleep when he comes into the house. We use a giant wire crate for our two Boston Terriers. By taking off the back of the crate you should now have the door opening into the house. This allows you access to the dog when you desire to bring him into the rest of the house. It also allows you to clean and add fresh blankets. The perfect setup is for the crate to lead out into the dog run enclosure. In this way you can protect the small dog from birds of prey (cover the run) or other animals. As with any dog run you want it on cement, and you want to have fresh water, shade, and shelter available. The dog can go out to exercise, potty, lie in a patch of sun, or just check out the surroundings. The dog also has access to the air-conditioning or heating that is in the house so that it stays warm or cool as needed. This is a great way to have a housedog in that you have a place to put them when you have guests over or when the housekeeper comes in. No more worries about doors being open or the housecat getting out the doggy door.

Even when you get to the point of leaving the crate door open and letting the dog have the run of the house; if you have a covered run, the housecat could get no further than the enclosure. You will need a door on the outside part of the run for cleaning access. When you first introduce the dog or puppy to the doggy door, you will probably have to tape it open for a few days. This gets the puppy used to the idea of going in and out of that space. This is obviously easier to do in warmer months of the year, but keep in mind that it is just 2–3 days and you should be able to gradually close the flap. The dog will learn to nudge it open with his head. If you have the type of door with the magnets, you will probably have to put tape in front of the magnets for awhile until the pup is more confident. If your puppy has difficulty learning to go out to go potty, you may be forced to use a small crate temporarily in order to force him to go out. Gradually your crate size can get larger.

The first step with a puppy is as easy as keeping them in this situation unless you are willing to be directly with him supervising. You can have him out as much as you want as long as you are there if he makes a mistake to correct him. If he goes to the bathroom in the house, you should first startle him with a clap of your hands and a "No," rattling a shake can if you have one handy or squirting him with the spray bottle (see chapter IV), all with the word "No" so that he learns the association of the word "No" with the negative. Next, take the mess to the place where he should go and show it to him there with praise. Go back and clean up the mess (without him present) with special pet stain cleaner so as to neutralize the odor. Dogs will often follow their noses back to where they have gone before and go again. You want to stop this before it becomes a vicious cycle, and that is precisely why you have to keep an eye on him when he is free.

3 Step method utilizing the doggy door

Set yourself up with the wire crate pushed up against the doggy door in an area that is not highly trafficked and is out of the way, such as a laundry room or a guest room. Avoid rooms where the dog will be staring at you often while you are eating or watching television, etc. Make sure that the area the dog goes out to is safe and secure. Temporarily tape the doggy door open with electrical tape until the dog is used to pushing the door with its nose to open. Depending on the age of the dog, you will typically want to use this system for 3 months before you go to the next step. The next step is to give the dog more room with the doggy door open, but not yet the entire run of the house. Either close the door to this room and give the dog just this room, or if the room is too large, use a temporary exercise pen for dogs or a fold out child pen to keep the dog just in one section of a large room. This should be in an area that has a tile floor or other uncarpeted surface. If there is carpet on the floor, you may have to temporarily use plastic runners on the carpet because dogs often go to the bathroom on absorbent areas such as carpet. It is important that you are training the dog how to live in the rest of house at this time. Use the "place" command (see chapter 5) and make sure you are observing the dog whenever he is out of his crate or confined area. This should be applied for another 3 months. At this point, your dog should have been conditioned for 6 months to use the doggy door and not potty in the house. He should be 8 months old or older, and he should be ready (provided you have been doing your training, to move further into the house with the doggy door open. You will want to go room by room and give him more and more freedom while still applying the place command and still monitoring his behavior.

You may at times have to take a step back prior to moving forward again. This is normal especially with a younger dog. Remember that the key to housebreaking is conditioning and giving freedom slowly but surely.

Crate training method

The crate training method gives the dog much less freedom of movement than the doggy door method, but it is the method of choice for medium to large dogs that will not be using the doggy door. The idea is to confine the dog indoors where he can be with you and get used to the sounds and smells that exist in the house without you having to follow his every move. Using the crate allows you to go take a shower, or get on a long phone call, etc., without having to worry about where the dog is or what it is doing. Using the crate training method you will bring the puppy or dog in whenever you want him in the house and position him where it is convenient for you. Do not respond and let him out if he whines. This will just serve to teach him that the more noise he makes the more likely you are to let him out. You want to teach him that his crate is a good safe place for him to be, so give him a safe toy to chew on and regularly give him a special treat when he goes in.

If his whining is too stressful for you, start him in an extra bedroom or garage or laundry room where you don't have to listen while he gets used to the crate. Gradually work the crate into your living space.

The key to crate training is to remember that you have total control of when the dog is in or out. You can use it for 20 minutes at a time or 8 hours at a time, dependant on the age of the dog and the timing (8 hours at a time would usually be at night while you are sleeping) as well as the weather conditions outside. For instance, our dogs are generally crated at night in the winter months when it is cold, and left out at night in the summer but crated during the hottest hours of the day in the air-conditioning away from the heat and flies. The proper use of the crate is to teach the dog to take a nap when indoors and for the owner to be able to regulate the potty sessions so that housebreaking can be facilitated. The crate is also an excellent device used for traveling so that the dog does not become a projectile in your car in case of an accident. When traveling to a hotel that accepts dogs, they are very happy to see you using a crate because they know that should you leave your dog in the room chances are he will not be able to destroy anything due to separation anxiety.

3 Step method using the crate

1. Introduce the puppy to the crate gradually for short periods of time. The crate should always be a positive place so give him something to chew on or a treat when you put him in. Put on some covering noise for him so that he isn't paying attention to your every move in the house. A television, radio, or soothing music is good for this purpose. Bring the puppy out and let him run around outside with supervision or in his puppy pen or dog run about every 20 minutes or so. The exception to this rule is if he is asleep. At this point, let him sleep until he wakes up. You can predict that when he wakes up, he will need to use the bathroom.

2. Your next step is to work up to keeping the puppy in the crate over night. If he is younger than four months old, you will have to get up with him once or twice during the night. If you cannot do this, you are best to make a puppy pen and leave the crate in it as a bed with the door open at night so that he can get up and potty himself. If you do take him out at night, do not play with him. This only serves to confuse the puppy into thinking you want him to have midnight play periods. It is best to try to give him some distance and be very quiet so that he will potty and go back to bed.

3. By four months of age, your puppy should be able to hold it all night. You will want to start to utilize the "place" command often while he is in the house and use the crate only when you cannot be with him or observe his behavior. You can also use the crate as a "place" for the dog with the door open while you are in the room. Simply shut the door when you need to leave the room. Moving into teaching the place command will set the dog up for the idea of coming inside and lying in the room you are in. As an older adult dog you will find the use of the crate will be just a convenience as the dog does not free wander or run through the house but rather goes from room to room near you and lies in his place.

Puppy Pens

A puppy pen as opposed to a dog run is a temporary device used to house a puppy when he is too young to spend much time out in a dog run due to weather or predators. A puppy pen should always be kept in a place that can be heated or air-conditioned and is free of drafts and flies. Whether it is constructed of chain link or simply and exercise pen that is reinforced, it should be able to hold the puppy and still have room for him to move around, potty (usually on shavings) and have an area for his crate, food and water. You

This wire exercise pen is useful for containing puppies in clean shaded and sheltered areas. They can easily be moved from place to place in the yard, on a patio, or any sheltered area.

do not want to feed the puppy in the shavings as he might inject them and get an obstruction so the pen needs to be large enough to divide in half: one half for potty area and the other for eating and sleeping. Common areas for this are basements, garages, laundry rooms, and covered patios, of course, depending on the time of year and weather conditions. Puppy pens are usually used in the transition period between 8–16 weeks. While the puppy is in its shot program and before crating all night may be a possibility. You can think of this like a babies play pen. The puppy pen is used primarily to keep the puppy out of trouble while at the same time keeping him in a reasonably safe and warm environment. A puppy left in a backyard will be destructive. He may chew on poisonous plants, fall in a pool or spa, chew on wires and receive an electrical shock, etc. If you take him out in your yard to explore under observation only, you can make the proper corrections necessary to teach him how you wish for him to behave while at the same time preserving your possessions (See Chapter IV). Let's look at life from our decidedly human point of view. We would not leave an 18 month old baby alone in the house or yard all day would we? Why not? Because he might hurt himself or our things? What might we do differently if we couldn't observe the child? Leave him in a playpen? Provide supervision? Why then should we imagine that a baby animal should somehow know how to conduct itself in a human household without supervision? When we give it some thought, we realize that expecting a puppy to leave our things alone and not get into trouble is about as reasonable as expecting a toddler to do the same thing. Puppies from 7–16 weeks of age are at the same stage in life as the toddler in diapers. They are going to explore their world with their paws and their mouths. Every object that is interesting to them will be moved, tested, and tasted. This is what makes the use of the puppy pen so important.

Baby gates

Baby gates have their useful applications in a house with a puppy much like they do with a baby. A baby gate can keep a puppy in a certain area of the house away from rooms that are carpeted and therefore more likely for the puppy to soil. It can also keep puppies away from rooms that have certain things in them that a puppy may be attracted to such as cat litter boxes and cat food. Baby gates allow you to spend time in a room with a puppy without having to chase them through the house. Baby gates, however, are not a substitute for observation. Left alone, the puppy may still potty on the floor, chew your cabinets or the leg of your kitchen table. The baby gate just serves to make it easier for you to contain the puppy while under observation.

Do not use Wee Wee Pads on the Floor!

Do not use cloth wee wee pads or newspapers on the floor in the home. This idea only serves to confuse the puppy about where it is supposed to eliminate. If you think about it from the puppy's point of view, you are teaching it that it is acceptable to go to the bathroom in the house. The puppy doesn't know the difference between a cloth wee-wee pad on the ground or a bath towel, bath rug, or door mat.

Dogs that are taught this way almost always have a problem soiling rugs and towels thereafter.

Conclusion

What confinement conditioning does for you is to allow you to get through the first two most difficult years of the dogs development with as little stress and destruction as possible. If you do your training properly and do not rely just on the confinement, you will have successfully conditioned the dog to live with the freedom of the house and the yard by approximately two years of age. You can at that point get rid of the confinement tools altogether if you wanted to. Most people, however, will use them as a convenience when the right situation occurs such as having guests over. The crate is a perfect travel tool and should always be used periodically so that if the dog should become sick or injured and has to spend time on bed rest, the dog will still be comfortable using this device.

IV. DOG BEHAVIOR AND PSYCHOLOGY

There is an entire book that could be written on dog behavior and psychology. Since we cannot cover every aspect in this work, we will attempt to address some key issues that a person needs to recognize in order to successfully train a dog. One of the biggest mistakes that people make in relationship to their dog is assigning human characteristics to them. This is called Anthropomorphization. It is no wonder that we humans look at everything from our own point of view. It is after all the only point of view we are familiar with. This causes a problem for us when we apply our own logic to an entirely different species. The problem when it comes to our canine friends is that they look at life from a distinctly canine point of view. To add to the difficulty for us television and movies both tend to play into this idea. Walt Disney movies that show animals talking in sentences and reasoning things out like humans tend to make us think that this is possible. So many dogs on film, in television shows, and commercials seem like they have even more reasoning ability than many humans.

In reality, dogs think like dogs, and people think like people. While we as humans cannot say that we know exactly how a dog thinks, we can say due to observation and scientific testing that dogs do not have complex reasoning ability. Examples of complex reasoning ability applied to a dog are statements such as: "He's mad at me because I left him at the groomer and that's why he came home and chewed up my shoes." Dogs don't get revenge like people do. They are not that calculating or vindictive. They simply act out of emotions such as boredom, frustration, and jealousy. They don't have complex thought patterns that can result in calculated behaviors such as planning to get revenge when he gets home by chewing his owners shoes. "He knows what he did wrong because when I get home and he's soiled the rug or chewed things up he ducks his head and puts his tail between his legs to show that he's sorry." Yes, it does appear that way, but what you are actually seeing is his understanding of the chaining of events not that they are WRONG. He soils the rug and he understands that the following event when you get home two hours later is you entering the house and yelling and threatening him. His bowing his head and tucking his tail is his way of reacting to you shouting, like he would react to a dominant dog. He is saying, "Okay, I understand you are the Alpha, you don't need to growl at me anymore." He is NOT, however, associating the act with the reaction. Right and wrong are human concepts, not canine concepts. In order to make the association such as this, the dog would have to be caught in the act. Dogs are born with a need to know the pack structure they are born into. This is a natural canine instinct. The dog having the same canine nature as the wolf has an innate pack mentality. The dog is naturally going to try to figure out where he falls into the pack. This is true whether the pack is canine, human, or a mixture. It does not mean that the human needs to rule over the pack with an iron fist. This couldn't be further from the truth. The true alpha leader is not only a leader with strong leadership traits but is also capable of great loyalty and affection as well. The alpha simply draws clear rules and regulations that the rest of the pack lives by. Following the rules, the pack also receives affection and loyalty from their leader. You can see this readily if you observe a wolf pack in action.

It is, however, important to note a few mistakes that humans often make in relationship to their dogs. For instance, you should always ask yourself as a human "who is being responsive to whom?" This is essential to dog owner relationships. Take this typical example:

You are sitting at your kitchen table, and your dog comes up to you and bumps your hand for attention. He wants to be petted. You in turn pet him. You've just told him that **HE'S THE BOSS**. In the dog's perception, the alpha always dictates the action. If you did just one thing differently, you change yourself into alpha position. Same scenario occurs, you ask the dog to sit, then you pet him. **YOU ARE NOW THE BOSS**. This is because even though he initiated the action to begin with, you made him respond to you before you rewarded him. In yet another example of canine and human differences, let's look at how dogs handle human children in the absence of the alpha. Most people don't realize that dogs have an acute sense of pecking order in the household. Dogs will not recognize children under puberty as being higher in the pecking order than themselves. This is why, in the absence of the adult pack leader in the house, the dog may decide that it is his or her job to correct the child if it misbehaves. Unfortunately, this correction is often directed toward the face as it would be with a puppy. The contact is usually around the eye area, and although it would not permanently scar a puppy, it is a very different scenario with a human child. This is precisely why as a parent or guardian, you never want to leave a child alone with a dog. Realize that where the dog is concerned, growling and biting are the only way it has of conveying displeasure. Humans tend to look at these actions as a betrayal of trust. The important point where these two convergent points of view are concerned is to establish pack order early with your dog. The best way to do this is through early training. It is so important to a dog to maintain its position in the pack that it will pay close attention to who is in charge and will gladly take over if the alpha leaves and he feels he is next in the pack order. He will also pay attention to whether he gets things first such as attention, food, and toys. Owners often cause fights between their dogs by unintentionally mixing up this process. For instance, two dogs named Duke and Jake live in the same home. Although it is difficult for two males to get along together, Duke and Jake have done pretty well as Jake was brought in as a puppy and readily accepted Duke who was 3 years his senior as the alpha dog. Now Jake has reached his teenage stage at 16 months and is beginning to challenge Duke. Their owners in an attempt to keep things "fair" between the two dogs tend to take turns with who gets attention and treats first. The effect this has on the dogs is to one day support Duke as alpha and the next support Jake. This causes ongoing fights for dominance between the dogs as the pecking order seems to be constantly changing, and the dogs have a natural desire to settle it. When the dogs fight, the owner tends to support the underdog and therefore this dog does not submit because the alphas seem to support his position. They keep going back and forth depending on who they (in their human wisdom) perceive to be right or wrong. This creates a never ending cycle that may result in them having to permanently separate the dogs or give one away. Another common misunderstanding between dogs and people is subordinate behavior that humans find irritating. Common behaviors that owners complain about are licking, groveling, and submissive urination. These are actually ways of the dog showing the owner that he or she is the supreme alpha and that there is no challenge for position. All of these actions are canine ways of showing respect. All you have to do to understand is to observe a wolf pack when the underlings greet the alpha. They lick his muzzle incessantly, pin their ears back, grovel, bow, roll over and expose their bellies and sometime submissively urinate. Humans are very often annoyed by these behaviors in their dogs, and they will show this by complaining in a low tone of voice. Guess what? This is exactly what a wolf does to show dominance. So you can probably guess what this means. Yes, you are actually reinforcing this behavior and making the dog grovel more! What does the alpha wolf do to end this scenario? Simple: He walks away. This signals that the ritual is over.

Reasoning Ability vs Trial and Error

As a human, you can be told how something works, reason out the facts, and apply what you have learned potentially without ever having tried it before. For a dog learning takes place by trial and error. This is how he is set up by nature. He learns that something that results in a good taste, feel, or food in his belly, etc., is a good thing and worth repeating. If it results in a bad taste, bad smell, scary sound, etc., then it shouldn't be repeated. This is one aspect of the dog's psychology that we can use to our advantage in training.

What this means in relation to training your dog is that if you have 100% control over the outcome of your dogs actions; you can quickly teach the dog how to add or eliminate a behavior based upon whether or not the action worked for him. Obviously, the next question will be "How do I do that?" When we began training dogs over 25 years ago, we noticed a glaring hole in training systems. Trainers had the "How To" methods on almost every subject except problem solving. When it came to problem solving most trainers had the disclaimer that you had to "catch him in the act," but at the same time they didn't provide for how you would do that. Obviously if you are at work 8–10 hours a day and your dog is at home chewing away like a termite, you can't catch him in the act. What makes training even more difficult is the fact that the more the dog does the act and enjoys it, the more he will repeat it. Therefore, if you only "catch him in the act" 10% of the time, and he is successful 90% of the time, he is going to keep on doing it! The owner is then chasing his own tail in attempting to correct an action that is happening 90% of the time when he is gone. It is most important at this point to realize how confusing it is to the dog when the owner comes home and is angry because of destruction. No doubt it is stressful to arrive home and not have any air-conditioning because the dog has chewed the wires, or you go to turn on the sprinklers and you have a geyser spring up in your backyard because the dog has chewed a sprinkler head. But let's really look at it from the dog's point of view. He's bored, you're not home, he has nothing to do, and chewing on your wires or your sprinkler head is no different to him than chewing on a stick. Now, you come home and start yelling at him. He doesn't understand a thing and so he does the only thing his pack mentality tells him to do. What is that? Grovel, roll over, bow, pee. And you think he is showing that he is sorry! Talk about messed up communication! We as humans have to keep in mind that there is no right or wrong here. There is no value of articles he chewed, no vendetta because you were at work. It is simply not that complicated! How would the dog know anything about vindictiveness or money? All he knows is that you come home angry, and he needs to show you that he is not challenging you for position. How sad for the dog! What a waste of time and emotions for you! This whole scenario is unnecessary and a complete waste of your time and possessions as well as your emotions. This is why we promote confinement conditioning as the key to your training solutions. Imagine the same scenario. You come home. Your young dog or puppy has been safely confined in his run with shade, water, shelter, and toys. You come home and turn on your air-conditioning (that works) and your sprinklers (that work). You let your dog out in the yard to play while you observe and play with him. You bring him into your air-conditioned home and spend the evening with him. You correct him when you need to and spend quality time with him. By the time he is an adult, he is free in the yard, and you can arrive home without your air-conditioning wires chewed and your sprinklers are still working. You use the run when you need to, but he is so well-incorporated into your life that you find yourself using it very little. How much easier on you! How much easier on the dog!

Ritual Behaviors

Dogs love rituals. People often notice this but fail to realize the importance to the dog. We notice that the dog always seems to know when it is dinner time even though he can not read the clock. He anticipates this time with joy and excitement, yet we are at a loss as to how he knows the exact hour of his feeding. Likewise, we might notice that the dog knows the exact hour of our typical arrival home from work or school. He may suddenly look up as if he is looking at a clock and run to the door in anticipation. When a cookie ritual is established after he eats his meal, the dog may run to the cookie jar or pantry with anticipation. Getting dressed may trigger a positive reaction in the dog because he knows that it is time for his daily walk, or a negative one because he knows that you are about to leave for work. The walk may lead to the dog romping in circles in anticipation or even bringing you his leash. Going to work may trigger moping around or even hiding in anticipation of you putting him outdoors for the day. All of these are examples of rituals that we establish either knowingly or unknowingly with the dog.

Examples of undesirable rituals that we set up are excessive barking, chewing, destruction in anticipation of events, or escape behaviors in reaction to or anticipation of events. The only way to permanently break these habits, all of which are formed by rituals is to change all or part of the ritual to break the chaining of the events in the dogs mind. Remember that dogs do not have complex reasoning ability but do react to the chaining of events and the emotions that are produced by those events.

Example: If your dog begins to run around and hide prior to your leaving home in anticipation of your putting him outside, in a dog run, or in a crate, make sure that you utilize those areas at various times throughout the day for a short time and with a positive association such as giving him a special treat, toy, or bone to chew on that he wouldn't otherwise receive in the house. Offer him these treats in association with the area in question for periods of 15–30 minutes, 2–3 times per day. This will help to make a more positive association with the location.

The next step is to anticipate his nervous reaction to your departure. Look for the triggers that set your dog into motion. It is usually something in your routine and timing, such as taking a shower or putting on your shoes. Dogs are good at knowing what time it is without the benefit of reading a clock. Work on switching up your routine as much as possible. This could mean putting him out earlier or putting him in a crate while you shower prior to putting him outside. Anything that makes the routine different will help to break the cycle and put you back in control. If barking occurs at feeding time, try changing the timing or what the dog is doing prior to the feeding. If you take him for a hike at feeding time, he will be so busy with the hike that he will not think about food until he returns. If you decide to feed him an hour prior to his normal feeding time, even though his mental clock goes off at his normal feeding time, he will not react because he is full. In this way you are resetting his ritual clock.

Teaching Positive Ritual Behaviors

While ritual behaviors can sometimes work against us, we can use this bit of psychology to our advantage in order to keep the dog understanding that we are in charge of his behavior and are, therefore, the Alpha in his life. Ask any credible trainer, and they will tell you that consistency and repetition are the keys to success in dog training. This is precisely due to the fact that dogs do not have complex reasoning abilities and to their love for rituals. This is set up by nature as a way for them to survive. Because of the dog's natural affinity for rituals we can teach him behaviors that we wish for him to carry out every day, such as stopping at doors and gates and waiting for a release word to exit, or coming in the house and lying only on his blanket or rug. As we teach puppies these behaviors in their first year of life, we notice that at some point, as long as the owners are consistent, the adult dog will automatically do these ritual behaviors without any need for coaxing or reminding on the owner's part. This is when you know that you have established a successful ritual behavior. Humans often commit errors when training a dog because they always think from a human point of view and apply the same logic to the dog. We tend to think that we can change things up and make life more interesting for the dog, when all this serves to do is confuse him. A good example of what we are talking about is changing where the dog's "place" is located. Let's say that for the past three years your dog has walked in the back door and turned right to go to his bed, which is located next to your reading chair. One day you decide to move the furniture around and you decide that his place will now be to the left, next to the couch. You have put a chair where his place used to be. Chances are that when he walks in the house, even with you trying to show him that his place has moved, he is going to turn right and go under that chair. While it is possible to retrain him to go to a new location, you shouldn't be surprised if you have to keep reminding him for awhile and correcting him for getting up and going back to his old place. This is because he has established a ritual behavior over the last few years that has become comforting to him. In the human mind the moving of the place is no big deal, because we have complex reasoning ability, which means that we can take a learned behavior and apply it in a variety of environments without a second thought. For the dog, each new location is monumental and needs to be practiced and ingrained into his pattern to become a ritual. The rule of thumb with dog training is to develop a style and stay consistent with it. The more simple and consistent the rules are, the easier it is for the dog to assimilate. Novice dog owners often make the mistake of trying to learn a number of styles of training at the same time and experiment on applying them on their dog. This is a big mistake, and very confusing to the dog. This would be the equivalent of you trying to learn several languages at the same time. You will likely only be able to pick up on bits and pieces of the systems you are trying to learn, and if you don't know it well, your dog certainly is not going to understand what you are trying to teach him. If you are excited about learning multiple styles and trying them out, you will want to have multiple dogs as your subjects and apply a single style to a single dog. Unless you are experienced in training dogs, learning multiple styles and applying them, even if only to one dog can be confusing. It is best to choose a style and stick with it.

The Pack Order Principal

As previously stated, it is of the utmost importance that you establish yourself as the pack leader with your dog. As the owner, this establishment of your control will make it much easier to live in harmony with the dog. Taking charge of the dog is not all about dominance, although dominance is one element. A true pack leader is also respected because he is fair, loving, and fun to be around. Very much like you would not respect an employer if he did nothing but boss you around all day, the pack does not respect a leader that is so one-dimensional. For you to really grasp what is and is not possible using the pack principal you must first understand what a *real pack* is and isn't. When we refer to a *real pack* we mean a *natural pack as it would appear in the wild*. For anyone who is seriously interested in learning about how real packs function, we would suggest learning about canine behavior with a biologist who studies real packs of wild dogs or wolves in their natural environment. We were lucky enough to be able to observe the Druid pack with a wolf biologist in Yellowstone National Park. We were amazed to see the precision with which the pack communicated with each other in the hunt. We witnessed them hunt and take down an elk, post guards on the kill, and then watch the ranking wolves eat and then howl to call the guards to eat. At other times, the wolves would howl to call to each other across ravines and announce the arrival of the Alpha. They would greet him with lowered heads and licks to the face which he accepted, but then, much like a talk show host when the applause lasts too long, he dismissed the excessive attention when it went on too long for his liking. First and foremost, you should be aware that a *natural pack* is a family unit. The pack generally consists of one Alpha male and female and their offspring from the last couple of litters. Depending on how good the hunting is and how harsh the winters are, there can be very large or very small packs. In general, the pack consists of brothers and sisters who help to provide the regurgitated food for the Alpha female and her new pups and later to help watch over the pups while the rest of the pack is hunting. In many ways, wolf packs are similar to large human families. Think of your family and how difficult it would be to bring someone new into your home to live with you. Bringing a new puppy home is a similar experience for the rest of your dogs. Because he is a baby, he is very likely to be accepted, just as you would probably more readily accept a baby into your household than an adult. There may be some jealousy in the pack, and it may take some getting used to, but the pack structure that has already formed remains intact because the puppy is no challenge to the rest of the pack until he hits puberty. It is, in fact, an entirely different matter when you bring home a new adult dog to fit in with your pack. This is not much different from an adult man or woman bringing home a member of the opposite sex and announcing that he or she will now be living with the family permanently. While there might be some people that would accept this, there are not many; and if they do agree to begin with, we could just wait around a little while and expect to see the fireworks start. Then there is the middle ground, which would be bringing in a new teenager to live with you. While he might need a home, everybody knows that teenagers aren't easy and can upset the apple cart quickly. Likewise, a teenage dog from about eight to eighteen months can be a pain in the neck for your other dogs to endure.

The point in the previous scenarios is that bringing in outside dogs to live together is *not a natural pack*. Since a pack is a natural family unit much like yours or mine, bringing home random dogs creates something of an orphanage where anyone who is dragged in must just assimilate and get along. Can it be done? Of course, given that you have the right blend of personalities and a clear pack leader. The failing in a pack situation is not what happens when the pack leader (human) is there and in charge; it *is what happens when he is not!* The alpha candidate will take over, and there will be a slight shift in pack order. The dynamics within a pack are ever-changing due to the aging of the animals within it, females who come in season and thereby create tension among the males, and the death of animals within the pack, which changes up the pack order. Just as happens when you put a random group of people together (like on reality television shows), dogs will form a pack hierarchy. Some will get along with their peers better than others. Over the years we have been in business, we have had several clients who have insisted on continually adding new dogs into their packs. Whether it be a puppy or an adult, these humans continue to insist that everyone must get along. When you put multiple adult males and females together, it stands to reason that sooner or later you will find one or two that just refuse to get along. Much the same, certain humans sometimes find it difficult to get along. These dogs generally have to be re-homed with owners who do not need to have multiple dogs. In a *natural* wolf pack there is only one Alpha male and Alpha female. When they get older, a son or daughter will step up to take the lead in the pack. If the succession is accepted by the old Alphas, the pack will let them live out their lives in peace. If there is a fight for dominance and the old Alphas do not submit their position, it may result in their deaths. Since this is what is at stake with your own pack it is important to know that if you insist on forming a pack of dogs (3 or more) you could be looking at veterinary bills or worse in the process of trying to make the arrangement work. There are three alternatives when you find yourself with dogs that do not get along in a pack:

1. Obedience train all the dogs and attempt to work them into a functional pack, accepting the risks that you are taking by doing so.
2. Place the dog that is difficult to blend into the pack in a more suitable environment.

3. Using kennels and crates, permanently separate the dogs that cannot be kept together. This is the option used by most dog breeders and dog sport enthusiasts in order to keep all of the dogs they wish without dealing with fighting and injury.

The truth of the matter is that those who love to philosophically tout the possibilities of the human transforming random dogs into a pack, either fail to realize or choose to ignore that there is nothing natural about random dogs forming a pack. In a true pack of wild dogs or wolves there is a certain level of mortality due to inner pack fighting and the infection of wounds resulting from the fighting. Pack membership is not an eternally blissful Shangri-La once formed. It is in fact full of peril for the dog or wolf that dares to challenge for position.

Behavior-Temperament-Trainability
Over our years of training dogs, we have learned to evaluate a dog's individual temperament and trainability in a very short time in order to accept or reject a dog into our training program. Another reason for evaluating a dog prior to training is to be able to council the owner properly on what is possible with their dog. It is our view that a dog's temperament is 60% genetic (a product of inherited traits) and 40% environmental.

There has been a great controversy in the dog training community with regard to this subject. This is, in fact, just a slight variation on the nature versus nurture argument. The reasons that we believe that genetics are slightly more important are these: If a dog is genetically deficient in a given area due to breeding (inherited traits), he may have weak nerves, be neurotic, or hyperactive, and no amount of training is going to help these deficiencies. Medications may help to manage some of these tendencies, but training will only help to teach the dog basic behaviors that assist the owner in handling the dog. Training will not be able to make the dog less nervous or hyperactive if genetic deficiencies are the source. If a dog is genetically sound, however, but has simply been under-socialized, neglected, or mistreated, *proper management and treatment of the dog, along with training can solve the problem.* The consequences of what the dog has been through can be reversed as long as the dog is put into a new environment and treated properly.

This analogy explains why it is so important to select a genetically sound animal in the first place. A trainer can only train what they are given to work with. No amount of training can make a dog into something it didn't have the ability to be from birth. Some owners will expect a trainer to be able to make a Siberian Husky be as precise in obedience and as protective as a German Shepherd. When asked why they think this should be possible, they often say that the breeds look similar enough that they figured that they both would be protective and just as easily trained. In fact, the Husky is a Nordic breed and was bred to pull sleds and be very sociable in groups. The German Shepherd was developed as a herding breed and guardian, which makes them much more willing to please and better suited for protection training.

In analyzing dogs over the years, we have developed the following classifications, which all dogs fall into to one degree or another. When dogs in the average categories (#5–#9) show traits of more than one number, we give them a half score. Thus a dog that displays some characteristics of a 7 and some of the 8 will be rated a 7.5. When we first observe a new dog in our consultation room, we look for overall health, vitality, sociability, or fearfulness. We observe the body language of the dog, as well as the owners, and the interaction between the two. We have a statue of a full-sized dog positioned right at the doorway and, unbeknownst to the owners and the dog, it represents the first test. Some dogs walk right past it without a sideways glance, others will freeze and bark or growl, a few will sniff at it and cower, and every once in awhile the poor statue is the victim of an all out attack.

When we actually sit down and observe the dog, we look for sociability, eye contact, attention span, willingness to please, willingness to take correction, fearfulness, boldness, response to a novel sound or object, noise shyness, hand shyness, and overall body language. We can often make statements about a dog that the owner interprets as psychic, but it really comes down to knowing how certain dogs of certain temperaments behave. The nervous system of the dog can be observed by how quickly and dramatically he responds to stimulus such as loud noises or novel objects such as our dog statue. Because the dog is coming into a new environment, if he is a nervous type he is going to show himself as such much quicker than he would in the comfort of home.

The Temperament Scale

The following is the scale we use to rate dogs when they come into our office:

#1 Mentally Retarded

This dog is a rarity to be presented for training, as most owners will realize automatically that the dog cannot be trained. It is not unusual for these dogs to also display physical abnormalities, such as a history of hydroencephilitis (which does not necessarily preclude trainability) and blindness. These dogs have often been saved from immanent death as puppies by well-meaning breeders. Nature would have otherwise culled them, as they could not feed themselves without human intervention. They may have been malformed in the womb or may not have received enough oxygen at birth. Many unsuspecting breeders find themselves nursing the puppy *back to health* just to find that the puppy will never truly be in *good* health. This makes the chore of keeping the puppy alive a permanent endeavor. Usually the dog becomes a bit of a doormat or lap wart in that it doesn't move around too much and cannot find its way to food or out of a room without help. Obviously no amount of training can change these circumstances. This dog is not a training candidate.

#2 Genetic Neurological

This dog is commonly brought in to see a trainer by owners that misunderstand what they are seeing in the dog. The owners often are hoping to be told what they want to hear, while on a gut level they know that the dog is not trainable. The problem that this type of dog has is not as obvious as #1 by simply looking at him unless you are trained to observe how a dog with neurological problems looks and behaves. In some cases, the dog will hold his tongue partially out of his mouth. The dog may show just the tip of the tongue or the entire tongue may dangle from the mouth. This will appear at times when the dog is not hot or stimulated in a manner that would explain such behavior. This dog is also extremely hyperactive and responds to every sound or stimulation by jumping towards the source of the stimulation. This dog seems to be in perpetual motion. Attempts to get the dog to focus or make eye contact just result in more motion on the dog's part. These dogs often shadow chase and become obsessed with novel objects, such as ceiling fans. This type of dog is often the result of inbreeding and often is excessively destructive, as it will constantly be looking for objects to vent their excess energy on. This dog should not be confused with a normal, active puppy. The #2 is wired **incorrectly, and no amount of training can solve this problem.**

#3–#4 Trainable (With Caveats)

This category of dogs is technically trainable in that they can learn basic obedience commands, but the risk for the trainer is that at the root of things the owner may actually want to change the dog's genetic makeup rather than teach it commands. *While training will make this dog easier to manage, it will not change the underlying genetic problem with the dog's nervous system.* There should be a good deal of counseling with the dog's owner regarding their expectations prior to starting the training process. A trainer can train a dog to ritual behaviors while not effecting the dog's reactions to things due to the genetically weak nervous system. In the following cases, the dog's weakness in the nervous system overrides its thinking ability. The dog reacts before it thinks and often sets off a number of behaviors that grow on themselves like an avalanche, depending on the level of stress the dog is under and his particular nervous system. For instance, it may jump, snap, pant, and whine all in rapid succession.

In most cases, owners of a dog with this condition really do want to change their dog's personalities through training. Since this is a genetic problem with the dog's nervous system, training will not cause the dog to calm down, and it is recommended that the dog be under medication to calm the nerves if training is attempted.

#3 Neurotic Fearful (Flight Response)
This dog will be presented as the equivalent of a scared wild animal. All new situations, novel objects, or loud sounds will be responded to with an attempt

to escape. The dog will generally appear with wide, bulging eyes, tucked and bowed head. Attempts will be made to run for shelter between the owner's legs or underneath a table or chair. These animals can be self-destructive when under stress. They often hurt themselves attempting to escape or will chew on their own legs or tails out of nervousness. Proper training for these dogs includes the use of anti-anxiety medication prescribed and monitored by a veterinarian. The suggested medication is Elavil (a human grade anti-anxiety medication), as these dogs are often brought in for training after hurting themselves because of separation anxiety. It is not uncommon for these dogs to jump through glass windows, tear at screens until their paws bleed, or chew on fences until their mouths bleed. In addition to medication, it is important that training is done in a place where the dog is exposed to a variety of other dogs and people who are non-threatening. These dogs may have to take training in small doses (using one week periods instead of three week periods, for instance) so that they have more time to adjust to training and a new environment. These dogs may refuse to eat in a kennel environment, and they may have diarrhea and/or vomiting issues. These are not life-threatening issues but should not be let go for a long period of time. This is why dogs that fit this description should be taken slowly and methodically through training. The medication should be administered and monitored prior to training for maximum effect.

#4 Neurotic Fear Aggressive (Fight Response)

Fight response to fear. This dog has to be handled carefully, as it can be dangerous to the trainer who has to handle it. This dog is similar in all ways to the #3, except that the way that it responds to anxiety is through aggression. This dog has a natural fight response when it is fearful. To this dog, the best defense is a good offense. The worst response that the trainer could give this dog would be to respond to aggression with more aggression. This would only serve to legitimize the dog's fear and support its aggression. This dog has to be handled with an abundance of patience, and it will generally select one or two people that it trusts, while often distrusting everyone else. As with the #3, Elavil is suggested under a veterinarian's care and supervision, and prior to beginning the training. As with the #3, training may have to be taken in small doses, and the training must be given in a very positive manner to be effective. A good experience for the dog can result in a very positive effect for the owners, although it is very important that the owners understand that the underlying problem is the poor nervous system, which cannot be affected by the training. In cases #3 and #4 the dogs can be improved with medication and training to the point where the owners will find it easier to live with the dog and accommodate the limitations of the dog. They will not, however, be able to expect the dog to become highly social; expectation should not be that the dog will be totally rehabilitated and be an acceptable member of society, because when their nervous systems are stimulated their ability to cope will still be diminished.

Trainable

The following dogs are in the acceptable training range without real difficulties or caveats. This does not mean that they will be equally easy to train as this depends on their individual breeds and personality types. In general, the more median temperament ranges will be the easiest to train.

#5 Trainable Non-Motivated (Freeze Response)

We have all known people that frustrate us because they are capable of much more than they attain and are completely unmotivated to use their capabilities. This is the best description of the #5. There is nothing wrong with the dog's capability to learn; he just doesn't care to apply himself. This dog is difficult to motivate. He doesn't seem to care about chasing a ball, playing tug, or working for food. He can take your praise and affirmation or leave it. He never shows any particular joy in working. In addition, this dog freezes when he is corrected. He does not do this out of stubbornness; he freezes out of fear of making a mistake. It is very important for a trainer to be able to recognize this, or the dog may be corrected for the freeze response out of the misconception that it is stubbornness.

This dog is worth training because the resulting behaviors make it easier for the owner to deal with him. In addition, the dog becomes better over time, as the training rituals are the same and the dog becomes comfortable with them. The fear diminishes, and the freeze response shrinks with it. This dog can be very frustrating for the trainer, as he never gives a happy tail-wagging performance. He simply exists and makes his way through the training process. When this dog is tested, he will show a minimal but sufficient amount of eye contact. He may appear to be bored with his new surroundings. The lights are on, but they are dim.

#6 Happy-Go-Lucky (Willing To Please)

This dog is, in many ways, the best obedience candidate. He is bright-eyed and sociable. He is interested in his environment. He has no particularly aggressive traits. He is a "good old boy." You will often see him cock his head during training as if he is trying to understand what you want. He has good eye contact and "soft eyes" that show no malice or mistrust. You will often see breeds such as Labrador Retrievers with this temperament. This dog is willing and often very motivated by toy or food reward. This dog is not often bothered by much in his environment and happily meets strangers.

#7 Slight Defense

This dog is very similar to the #6 with the exception that he is a little more guarded. He assesses his environment and whether or not he can trust. He is defensive enough that he is a bit more protective of his owners and environment than the #6, but he is still very willing to please. You will see a few more of the guardian breeds in this category, such as German Shepherds and Dobermans. This is the first of the categories where the dog can be protection trained to Level 1 defense, the category where they can bark a warning and act defensively while still remaining a good companion dog with a somewhat subservient personality.

#8 Companion Protection

This dog is willing to please, but also has a very assertive personality. Because he has a strong personality, he will also be more stubborn to work with in obedience. Pack structure is always a factor with this dog. If his owner does not take the leadership position, he will. This dog has what it takes to defend the home with physical force. This is the prime candidate for home protection training because he is willing to submit himself to an Alpha leader but is always strong enough to take charge if he needs to. His eye contact will be strong and watchful, but not offensively aggressive.

#9 Alpha Candidate

This dog is willing and able to take the Alpha role and takes a strong owner to be able to keep him in a lesser position. In the right hands he can be a wonderful dog, but with a more submissive owner he can be a nightmare. This is the typical temperament of a police dog. When tested, this dog gives full eye contact. He is ready for a challenge, and his body tends to lean forward as if he is ready to spring. When he is tested or challenged, he will easily rise to the occasion. He may be very aggressive when the owner is present in order to protect his owner, vehicle, or home. This is especially true if the owner has no control over his behavior and he has taken on the Alpha role. This dog should be trained when young, and in most cases, males should be neutered if not owned by a professional handler. Trainers training older dogs of this level should do so with caution and may have to use a double leash or muzzle for safety.

#10 The True Alpha

The #10 is just as rare to see as the #1 is. Most dogs who people think are Alphas are actually Alpha Candidates. The true Alpha will die before he submits position. No manner of training will break this dog's desire to dominate once he is an adult and established in this position. This dog is extremely dangerous as an adult to the person who attempts to train him. This dog, while trainable when very young, will erupt into a dangerous dog when he hits puberty. The only place for this dog once he has achieved his Alpha status is in area protection. He will be approachable by those he accepts into his pack, but they will not be able to tell him what to do or put him into a subordinate position. This dog will even bite the owner if he tries to assert himself over the dog's food, toys, or position.

V. PUPPY PRE-SCHOOL (2–4 MONTHS)

Puppy Pre-School should be upbeat, fun, and done with food and toy reward.

You have your adorable puppy and you are now ready to embark on your training mission. There are some important things that you should take care of from the very beginning: veterinary care, nutrition, safety, and general welfare.

The Three Basics
Health

Have the puppy examined—an overall health check—as soon as you can. Speed is important just in case some health defect is found that will force you to return the pup. You don't want the family to become too attached to the animal in the event this should happen. It is also important to get your puppy started on the vaccination schedule that your veterinarian recommends.

Talk with your vet about diet considerations, supplements and vitamins, as different breeds require various foods and supplements. We have found that if you use top-quality, meat-based dog foods such as chicken or lamb with rice, rather than corn or **wheat** fillers, with twenty-six to thirty percent protein, most supplements will not be necessary.

Safety

Unfortunately, safety is often overlooked by many owners. Safety involves having all dangerous substances removed from the puppy's grasp. It also involves proper confinement, so that the puppy does not get hit by a car, drown in a pool, or become lost, stolen, or attacked by another animal.

Puppies will chew anything. Check your home and yard for poisonous plants. Be especially aware of plants such as Poinsettias, which are popular at Christmas time as decorative plants, but can cause severe illness or death to a puppy. Remove cleaning fluids, electrical cords, and small ingestible items. The same safety concerns that apply to a human baby will apply to your puppy.

Confine the puppy in a safe area—dog run, puppy pen, or safe, confined area away from personal things that you don't want destroyed.

Welfare

Welfare is looking out for the general needs of the puppy. You should be sure to provide him with fresh water that is changed daily, fresh food that is not left out (so as to prevent insects and birds from getting to it), plenty of shade so that he does not suffer from heat exposure, and shelter from the wind and rain. He should be kept in a well-ventilated area that is free from drafts or dampness. Keeping him in a well-lit area in the daytime also is essential for his development. You do not want to keep him in a dark room or in a garage that is not illuminated during the day. A light in the room can be sufficient, however, as direct sunlight is not always possible. It is also a good idea to put a television on near the puppy to get him used to a variety of noises. This is especially important if you are not able to take the puppy out yourself during the day because you are at work or otherwise occupied.

Bringing the Puppy Home

It is important to understand that it is necessary to lessen the stress of separation from the litter as much as possible when you bring the puppy home. The optimum time for homecoming is in the seventh week of life. The reason for this is that the puppy will enter the critical fear period when it is eight weeks old. This critical fear period lasts until the twelfth week of life. During this time, things that frighten the dog can have a long-term impact on it. If you can have the puppy home for at least 3 days prior to this period, the puppy will be much more settled during this critical period in his life. Bring the puppy home early in the day if possible in order to allow adjustment to new surroundings before the puppy is left alone at night to sleep. You should purchase the same food that the puppy has been used to eating at the breeder's home. Changing the dog's diet right away is not a good idea. The puppy will be under enough stress from his new environment as it is and changing his diet will almost ensure that you will have housebreaking problems to deal with as well. A puppy's digestive system is delicate and takes time to adjust to new foods. If you do choose to change foods, you should make the change at least three weeks down the line and at twenty-five percent intervals over several weeks.

The crate is an excellent tool from which the puppy can view his world at a safe distance. The crate can be moved from place to place in order for the puppy to get used to several different areas of the house. The crate also allows the puppy to see, hear, and smell all of the normal activities and people that he will be expected to exist with. If there are cats in the house or small children that may run and scream, these will all be things that the puppy will have to become accustomed to. When the puppy no longer seems frightened by its surroundings you may want to, with supervision, bring the puppy out to investigate the things he has seen.

Puppy Preschool

Puppy owners are often confused about when they should start training the pup. Many have heard different ages quoted by various trainers, ranging anywhere between eight weeks and one year of age. The multitude of options can be confusing.

The truth is that you should begin training as soon as the puppy is adjusted to your home environment, but only at the level that is age appropriate for the puppy. You won't expect the same level of concentration from an eight-week old puppy as you would from a four-month old, and you wouldn't expect the same concentration from a four-month old that you would from a nine-month old, and so on. Even though your nine-month old may be as large as an adult dog, don't expect him to act mature.

As with children, every age has its stages. An eight-week old puppy is very much a preschooler. They can learn what commands mean, but within the constraints of a very short attention span. At four months of age, the puppy begins to lose its baby teeth and adult teeth begin to appear. Much like a Kindergartener, this signals a readiness for basic elementary school training. Puberty sets in for your dog at around nine months of age, and this is an appropriate time to review elementary training and advance to off-leash training.

Much like a teenager, this is the time where the puppy may turn a deaf ear to your commands. At twelve to eighteen months of age your dog can progress to advanced obedience, agility, or protection, or any other advanced work you may have in mind. This is the equivalent age to high school. From eighteen to thirty months a dog in training for a certification or title will most likely perfect its skill and be ready to take on the challenge of competition or work as a service dog. This can be related to college and grad school.

Most people involved in dog sports, competitions, or service dog work (police or search and rescue, etc.) will tell you that they do not consider a dog ready to perform to peak ability until it reaches the age of two and a half years old.

Starting Your Puppy Off Right

Your attitude with a puppy should always remain positive. You don't want to apply stress to the puppy. There will be a lot of time ahead for you to perfect what you are teaching. Right now, your single most important task is to give the puppy a positive view of what it means to work with you as a handler. This is not really obedience training in as true of a sense as it will be later, but rather obedience pre-conditioning.

We will be using food to motivate the puppy. When food is used properly, you will eliminate all stress on the puppy. You want the puppy to look forward to seeing the leash and to associate it with the fact that there will be reward and interaction with you. The collar you will be using at this stage should be a flat leather or nylon type.

You will want to start with four basic commands: heel, sit, come, and down. We do not use "stay" with this age group, as it requires an attention span that is very difficult for this age group. You may use any language that you are comfortable with as long as you remain consistent. You will want to practice at a time when the puppy is normally hungry, such as prior to feeding times. Remember that the food represents the same thing to the puppy as something that would motivate you (such as money), so you want to use something that is really appealing, such as chicken or a hot dog. Find something that the puppy really likes, but which is not available to him in his daily feeding. This food item should be small enough to be quickly chewed and not something that is large and crunchy. If the puppy takes too long to consume it, he will forget the lesson you are teaching.

For the puppy in preschool, the "sit" and "down" commands will be the easiest to master. This should be done in an environment that the puppy is used to, such as your kitchen or family room. When you get to the movement commands, you will need more room to move freely. Depending on your living environment, this may be in the house or outside in an area that the puppy is used to. You do not want to try this in an area that is new to the puppy, as his natural instincts will be to explore the new environment.

Sit

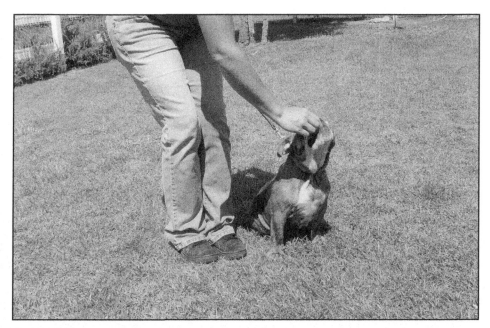

When teaching the puppy to sit pull the food up over the head so that by trying to obtain the food the puppies rear end naturally goes to the ground.

Hold the tidbit of food in front of the puppy's nose and raise it to slightly above his head, so that he has to tilt his head back to see it. Command "sit" in a calm, positive voice. The puppy's rear end should naturally go down into a sit position as he looks up at the food. As soon as the puppy sits, praise him with "Good Sit" and give him the treat. Remember always to be positive and offer lots of praise. Do not get frustrated and start pushing and pulling at the puppy. There is no hurry. If you start to get frustrated, just put the puppy away and try again another day.

Down

Hold a little tidbit of the treat in front of the puppy's nose and lower it to the ground a little forward

From the sit position pull the food forward toward the ground to get the puppy to lay down effortlessly.

between the puppy's paws. Let the puppy follow the food down to this position.

His rear end may stay in the air. Gently push his rear down, but do not release the food to him until his entire body is in the down position. Command "Down" and release the food to him if the entire body is down. If he pops up in front, be patient and start again. Do not give the food to him unless the entire dog is in the down position. You should not say "lay down" or "get down," as this only confuses the dog and complicates your training later. When he does assume the "down" position, praise him with "good down" and stroke him along the spine. Allow him to get up again if he wants to. Do not fight to keep him in the down position at this point, as this would be the "stay" position, and the puppy does not have the attention span for this yet.

Heel

The heel command involves teaching the puppy to walk on a leash on your left side (which developed as a matter of tradition due to most people being right handed and using this hand for a weapon) with the dog sitting automatically when you stop.

Teaching the puppy this command requires a fairly large area so that you are not walking in circles. Walking in a circle makes it more difficult to teach, because the puppy will not be able to move as freely.

You will want to downplay the leash and use the food in front of the puppy's nose so that he moves forward toward the tidbit without thinking about the leash. If the puppy realizes that he is being pulled along by the leash, he will probably panic and pull back. This creates a negative association with the leash and should be avoided. In order to practice the heel command properly, place the puppy on your left side and use your left hand to hold the tidbit in front of his face. Use the puppy's name followed by the command (for instance: "Duke, heel") and begin to move forward, keeping the tidbit centered in front of his face. While walking even a few steps say "Good Heel" and stop, lifting the tidbit up over his head, but keep it within range of his mouth. As he tilts his head back, command "sit" and then praise him with "good sit" as he puts his rear to the ground. Reward him with the tidbit. Do this just three times, taking a few steps each time. Give him a lot of praise and reward him each time.

Teaching the heel command is simple when you lead the puppy using food in front of her nose.

Make sure that you quit while you are ahead and while he is still enjoying it. If you do too much at once, he is likely to tire of this experience and become less willing to perform. With a puppy, you will want to work on short successes.

Come

Now that the puppy is fully aware that you are holding a tidbit, move back and away from him. Call the puppy by name and say "Duke (substitute his name), come". Hold out the treat towards him to show him that if he comes to you, he will receive the treat. Draw him towards you by backing up a couple of steps as

When calling the puppy to you show her the food and lead her toward you.

he comes towards you and praising him the entire way ("Good Come"). When he gets in front of you, lift the treat over his head and slightly back as you did in the heel command, only this time he should be sitting directly in front of you. Command "Sit" and, when he does, quickly praise and reward him with the tidbit.

Pre-Training for Advanced Applications

While puppies need to mature into being able to do advanced work such as retrieving, search and rescue, tracking, and protection work, there are also many activities you can participate in with your pet that will be enjoyable for him. Things that the puppy experiences as positive and fun will develop into habits that can be utilized later on. Examples of these games are:

Retrieving

Playing little retrieving games with the puppy using a small toy is an excellent way to build up the retrieving desire that can be used later in obedience, hunting and field training, or service dog work. A puppy's natural tendency when you toss a toy towards him may be to pick it up and carry it away. One of the best ways to get him to bring it to you is to have a second toy that you gain his interest with after he picks up the first toy. In this way, he is always in interaction mode with you and not thinking that you want to take his toy. Start with soft toys, and as he progresses in the game over time, you can use a variety of objects. Always keep it fun!

Tracking

Find a location in your yard where the earth is a bit soft or the grass is a bit high, and you can make a fun game out of tracking your puppy just a couple of paces at a time. The early morning, when the ground is still damp is a good time to do this. Take a few very small pieces of hot dog and start by laying a scent pad in an area about two feet square. Stomp around in this area, shuffling your feet so that the ground smells disturbed and will have the scent of your feet. Put some pieces of the hot dog in this area so that the puppy will pick up your scent as he searches for the little pieces of food. Then step off a couple of paces, heel to toe, in one direction, making sure that you disturb the ground under your feet but not to the sides. Lay pieces of hot dog in your tracks. At the end of two or three paces put several pieces of hot dog as his ultimate reward. As he gets good at doing this for just a few paces, add one more step at a time. Make sure that his ultimate reward is at the end. This can eventually be his toy, so that you can play a rewarding game of tug or fetch when he is done. In this way, he will learn that following your footsteps is rewarding and that the ultimate reward is a game with you. Always use the same command consistently for tracking.

Searching

Start by having a favorite family member hide behind a couch or in an easy area for the puppy to go to them. Have the person hiding look out from behind the couch and call the puppy's name. While holding the puppy, ask him "where is he?" and have the person behind the couch peak his head out and then pull back. Tell the puppy "search" and let him go. When the puppy runs behind the couch to find the hidden person that person should praise him and give him a treat. Continue making this game just a little bit harder each time, until the puppy can run to find the person in different rooms and hiding behind and inside various areas.

Protection

Playing tug is very important for dogs that will go into protection training. You can start playing tug with something as little as a wash cloth. Simply roll it up and tie it off at both ends with a shoe lace. Eventually you will move him up to a larger towel, jute rag, and then jute toys, rope tugs, and finally actual protection equipment as he gets older. Make sure that you put away the tugs when he is losing his baby teeth (at between 4–5 months of age). Pulling a tooth out during a game of tug can be painful and therefore decrease the willingness of the puppy to bite hard while playing this game. The puppy should always win when he plays tug. Never pull the tug out of the puppy's mouth. If you want to get the tug from him, distract him with another toy. Always use the same word when the puppy bites.

Command Words

Command words can be literally anything that you want them to be. The rule of thumb is to keep it short and distinct from other commands. You can use English or any other language, as the dog does not know the difference. Some people like to use another language or code words so that others cannot speak commands to their dog. This is purely a matter of personal preference, and the only rule of thumb (other than keeping the commands to one word each) is that they should be simple for you to remember. It doesn't work well if you are confused as to which words mean what.

Puppy Problem Solving

Problem solving for a puppy who is in the age range of 2–4 months is a little different than problem solving for the older puppy or adult dog. You should keep in mind that the puppy is going through its critical fear and socialization periods at this age, so you do not want to do anything to make him fearful.

You can go a long way towards solving problems with young puppies by not allowing a problem to develop in the first place. The best way to do this is to keep the puppy out of trouble using confinement conditioning. The single most common mistake people make with puppies is allowing them to have too much freedom too soon. When this happens the puppy is obviously going to have accidents in the house and get into things that he shouldn't. The rule of thumb with this age group should be that the puppy will be confined to a puppy pen or crate whenever you can't directly supervise him. If the puppy is out of the confined area, someone in the family must be responsible for what he is doing at all times.

Housebreaking

This is without a doubt the biggest issue in a house with a new puppy. Some people expect that the puppy will in short order announce when he needs to go out. This is rare to have happen right away, simply because the puppy does not know any better at this point. The only way to teach him is to regulate where he is when he needs to go and prevent him from going in the wrong area. This requires that he be kept in a crate, where he is less likely to soil his own bedding, or in a puppy pen, where he has the room to move around and go into an area with shavings to potty. Going to the bathroom in shavings will teach him to seek out a more natural scent when he needs to use the bathroom and make him less likely to seek out your rug. Puppies naturally are attracted to absorbent areas when they need to go, so shavings are a good solution. Don't make the mistake of using the cloth pads that are sold in pet stores. These serve to confuse the puppy into thinking that it is okay to go in the house. These cloth pads also teach the puppy to seek out similar material for potty purposes, so, before you know it, you will be squishing through your bathroom rugs and door mats because they look and smell similar.

When the puppy makes a mistake in the house, you should be right on top of him correcting him immediately. Clap your hands to startle him and give a loud "no." Do not strike him or rub his nose in it (grandpa's old method), as this does nothing but make the puppy afraid of you. Simply take the puppy to where he should go and let him finish. Take a paper towel with whatever urine or fecal matter he has already eliminated to the proper area and set it there. He will make the connection that this is the proper area only if this is done in a timely manner. If you are not watching and you do not catch him in the act, you will not make the connection for him and your opportunity will be lost. An additional way to make a negative association for the puppy is to have a squirt bottle with 50% white vinegar and 50% water on hand. The bottle should be set to stream so that you can squirt it towards the puppy's nose when he is doing something wrong. Avoid the eyes as this will burn. A well placed squirt when you say "no" while catching him in the act should cause him to shut down the bladder movement, make your point, and give you time to grab him and take him outside. One very simple way to begin housebreaking a puppy is with the use of a crate pushed up against a doggy door that leads to an outside pen. This is usually used for small-to-medium sized dogs that will eventually have the run of the entire house. It can certainly be used for large dogs as well if the size of the doggy door in the wall is not prohibitive to the owner. This door should be placed in a non-traffic area of the house, such as in a bedroom or bathroom wall. It is preferable that the area around the doggy door is not carpeted, as it will make the second step in this process much easier. You should avoid putting it in a door that you actually use, because the crate will be blocking the door for a period of time while the puppy grows. This is the only time that we suggest using a wire crate. Wire crates are made in many different fashions. You can generally remove a side or back to the crate, and some even come with multiple doors. You will want to place the door to the crate facing into the house so that you can access the puppy easily. Take the back off of the crate, use the second door, or cut a hole into the crate large enough for the puppy to access the doggy door. The final option is sometimes the better solution, as the wire protects the wall from the puppy chewing on it. The outside area should be safe and free from danger. The area should be shaded and covered if birds of prey are an issue. The most preferred surface is cement, as it can be easily cleaned and disinfected. You may need to temporarily tape (using electrical tape) the doggy door open, so that the puppy will learn to go in and out at will. Eventually, you let the door down further and further until the puppy is willing to push it open himself. This process usually takes 3–7 days in total.

Chewing

Chewing is something that puppies do naturally. Like human babies who explore their environment with their hands and mouths, the puppy does the same. You can't expect a puppy in this age group not to chew. What you can do is control what he has access to for chewing purposes. This is why the puppy pen is so important. Since you cannot possibly watch him twenty-four hours a day, you will need to put him in a safe environment so he does not chew on electrical cords and things that could hurt him. In this way you are also protecting your things from him. When you do have him out, under supervision, make sure to have three or four toys near you so that you can replace the inappropriate items with appropriate ones. No corrections should be applied for chewing at this age unless the puppy becomes relentless in his pursuit of a particular item. At this point you can use the same squirt bottle that we mentioned previously in order to prevent chewing. Make sure you always use the word "no" when squirting him so that he can make the association with the correction word.

Playful Biting and Jumping Up

Playful biting and jumping on people should be handled with this age group in much the same way as the chewing problems. This is much less of a problem when you use a puppy pen and make the choice to deal with the puppy when you can. Again the puppy is simply exploring its world by using its mouth. Giving the puppy a toy when it is trying to chew on your arm or your toes is the best distraction. Again, if the puppy is persistent, you can use the squirt bottle. Don't overdo the squirt bottle. However, but rather save it for times when the puppy just won't quit.

One of the greatest difficulties with puppies occurs when there are very small children in the house. Children usually want to play with the puppy, but will often run away and scream in terror when they discover how sharp that puppy's teeth are. Small children should only be allowed to play with the puppy when directly supervised by the parents. Chase games should not be allowed because they always lead to problems. If the children chase the puppy, they will in affect be teaching the puppy to run away, and this will affect the training adversely later on. If the puppy chases the child, it is a natural reaction for the puppy to nip at the child's heels or diaper when he gets to them. This will result in the child crying and hitting at the dog. This sets up a negative scenario that often results in the punishment of the puppy for doing something that comes naturally, as this is how he would play with another puppy. It is recommended that the parent always supervises the play between children and puppies and makes sure that the duration of the time they are together is short and stays positive for both of them.

Conditioning

It is important to remember for this age group that you are not *solving problems*. You can not permanently solve puppy problems at this age any more than you can expect a two to three year old toddler to act like an elementary-school age child. A puppy of this age is a work in progress. Don't lose your patience and strike the puppy. You will need to put yourself into the mindset that you will be moving along to the next step when the puppy is four months old. This is similar to your understanding that your child will be entering a new phase in his or her life when he or she enters elementary school.

VI. PUPPY ELEMENTARY SCHOOL

An untrained dog can pose a danger to your safety.

(4–8 MONTHS OF AGE)

When a wolf cub is four months old, it comes out of the protected den area and begins to explore the environment and romp after its mother, learning to catch rodents and other small creatures. The loss of the baby teeth and the acquisition of adult teeth mark the period where the cub is ready to eat solid foods on its own and when it no longer needs either its mother's milk or regurgitated foods. For our domesticated canines, the loss of the baby teeth represents the time when the pup is ready to learn what you expect of him around the house with regards to manners and obedience. This is elementary school age for pups.

There will be eight different lessons that we want to teach the pup at this age. Three of these lessons have to do with manners around the house. They include: Coming in the house and lying down in "place," stopping at the boundaries of the yard, and not entering a street unless released to do so (boundary control). And to stop when entering through doors and gates and wait for a command to either go in or come out (door crashing). In addition, five basic obedience commands should be learned. These are: Walking on the leash at the "heel," which is typically on the left hand side, without pulling. He should automatically sit when you stop and change pace and direction with you. The sit command and down command will be taught from a stationary position, and the stay command will be taught with distractions. In basic obedience training, these commands will be practiced on a six-foot leash as well as a thirty-foot long line to teach the dog to respond to you from a distance.

Selecting a Dog Trainer and Method

Before you begin training your dog, you should research the trainers and methods that are available in your area. Around large, populated cities you may have many choices, whereas in more rural areas you may have very few. As mentioned previously, you should decide upon a method that you believe in (and can stick with) prior to your selection. Many people make the mistake of selecting on impulse and then regret the decision that they have made afterwards. There are many training styles, all of which differ a great deal from one another, so you should be cautioned that a good deal of research should be conducted from the time that you make the decision to purchase the puppy right up until the time that you select your trainer. Methods can range from the passive "click and treat" method to the very aggressive "shock collar" method. As in most areas of your life, moderation is generally the best method, and finding someone whose methods can work for both passive and aggressive breeds is generally your best bet. There should always be a large amount of praise and reward available to your dog in any positive, motivational training style. At the same time, it is important to know that discipline (not abuse) is as necessary with dogs as it is with children.

In addition to the method selected, you will have choices of how the training is done. These choices can range from group classes to private lessons at the trainer's facility, or private lessons in your home. A very popular way of training dogs today is in-kennel training (wherein the dog stays at the trainer's facility for training), but this approach should only be selected if there are lessons offered for the owner with the dog afterwards. In our training program, we offer both in-home lessons and lessons for the owner at our facility following the training. This has the benefits of all of the styles of training combined. The in-kennel form of training is popular because it is the only way that owners can train their dog without having to put in the daily training time themselves. With so many people commuting long distances to work on a daily basis, we have found over the nearly three decades that we have been training dogs, that a lack of commitment from owners is the single biggest obstacle to adequately training a dog.

With an in-kennel program it is the trainer's responsibility to get the initial part of the training accomplished. This should then be followed by a demonstration of what has been taught, as well as a lesson for the owner. Most kennels will also have follow-up policies that vary from location to location, but we feel that it is very important for the trainer to visit the owner at their home at least one time during this process. This is because many times there are environmental issues that need to be addressed, such as fencing, elimination of barrier frustrations, house breaking issues, etc. At K-9 Companions, we allow the clients to come back up to once a month for the first year after the in-kennel lessons are completed to receive a free brush-up. We will also board their dogs when they are out of town and brush up the training at the same time. You should look for these sorts of benefits, which make paying a higher price for in-kennel training worth it throughout your dog's life.

The purchaser of a training system should proceed with caution, because, as with any other purchase, much of your satisfaction will depend upon the integrity of the company that you choose. Not all training facilities are equal, in fact far from it. Because there is no standardized credentialing process for trainers in this country, there are no quality assurances in choosing a trainer. In addition, you will find that trainers come from a broad variety of backgrounds. Common forms of training experience are: People who have apprenticed under professional trainers and/or taken trainer's certification courses from professional trainers, former military or police K-9 trainers, competitors in dog sports, or other forms of training competitions. There are college courses that include dog training as part of the curriculum, but none offer the practical experience that trainers get training hundreds of dogs personally when they apprentice at an actual training facility. In our opinion, this is, hands down, the best experience a trainer can have. The least favorable would be the online college courses that are available; while they offer a fancy certificate at the end, they offer very little, if any, practical experience along with the certification.

Another very important factor to look at while selecting a trainer and facility is how long they have been in business and whether or not they own the facility themselves. The answers to these questions will give you insight into both the trainer's experience and stability. Obviously, if someone is just starting out in the business, they are more likely to make mistakes and lack the experience necessary to deal with all of the situations that might arise. The stability factor serves as insurance for you. If a trainer is working out of someone else's facility, there is less assurance for you that they will remain at this location. There is also the question of who is ultimately responsible for the care and safety of your dog. Is it the owner of the kennel or the trainer that is going to be responsible if something should happen to your dog while in their care? Ask the trainer just how many people will be taking care of and training your dog. Who are these people and what kind of training do they have? Find out how many dogs are being trained on a daily basis and how many trainers are training them. This is an important element to your decision making process, and if there is only one or two people doing the training, something like an illness or injury can really impact the results you get from the training. It is also more beneficial to your dog if there are several people training, so that your dog does not become bonded to just one person. At our facility we have over a dozen people caring for and training the dogs. If someone is ill or injured, the other employees can easily take up the slack. We have seen several instances in facilities with few, if any, employees where the activities have come to a halt due to an unexpected illness.

Group Classes

Group Classes are typically offered by organizations such as your local Parks and Recreation Department or Pet Stores. They are typically the lowest-cost training on the market and, as such, offer a limited time for participation. A typical group class may involve one or two dozen participants and their dogs all being instructed by a single instructor. This type of training is generally effective for people who have trained dogs before and want a refresher or something structured enough to keep them on track. Dogs with easy-going temperaments, who are not difficult to train in the presence of other dogs and people can generally do well in classes like these. The type of people who do not do well in these classes are those with hectic schedules, who are unable to be consistent about showing up at the class and following through with practice on a daily basis. The way that these classes are generally structured prohibits people from making up the classes that they miss and those who do not show up on a weekly basis tend to fall behind and become discouraged. Dogs that are difficult to handle around other dogs and strangers can become disruptive, and many times they are asked to leave the class so that the other participants can continue without the distraction caused by such a dog's behavior. A group class is usually structured to be held at the same time each week for approximately an hour. The instructor will usually stress that homework must be done daily for thirty to forty minutes per day over the length of the course, which is generally six to eight weeks. Problem solving in these courses is usually minimal and involves verbal advice from the instructor, which students then attempt to implement in their homes.

Private Classes

Some trainers will offer private classes that include only you and your dog or a group of friends or family that you might put together. The benefits of this type of training are that you have the instructor's time to yourself and he or she can concentrate on helping you and your dogs with your specific needs. Another benefit of this type of training is that you can generally reschedule your lessons if you cannot attend at the designated time. Like the group class, you must practice your homework daily to have success with this type of training, but the additional benefit is that you can sometimes take longer between lessons to get the homework done because of the ability to reschedule the lessons with the instructor. As with the group classes, the problem-solving ability is minimal because the instructor is never at your home. Expect to pay two to three times as much as you would for group classes, since you have the instructor's complete attention.

In-Home Training

In-home training has a couple of benefits for convenience and problem solving that group and private on-field lessons do not. Instead of spending the time driving to the trainer for classes, the trainer comes to your home. The benefits of this to your convenience are obvious. Another benefit is that the trainer can help you on a weekly basis with your problem-solving issues because they are right there in your home to help you make necessary changes. Like the group and private class options, you are still required to work with your dog on homework daily to keep the training moving forward.

The biggest drawback to in-home training is the lack of socialization around other dogs and people. Many of the issues that people wish to work with through training have to do with the dog's actions around strangers and other dogs. Training in the dog's home environment does nothing to help these issues. The other factor with in-home training can be the price. Since the trainer is traveling to your home, they are going to charge a significant price for time, gas, and mileage. Like most things, you will have to determine whether your convenience is worth paying more for the luxury of your trainer coming to you.

In Kennel (Boot Camp) Courses

As previously stated it is very important when you decide to opt for an in-kennel course (Boot Camp is our trademark for this type of course) that you choose carefully and wisely. You are turning over your dog to someone else to care for and train. In our opinion (after training for almost three decades), this course is the most successful. This is because we have control over the fact that the dog will be trained every day. The fact that the dog is being trained by professional trainers, and therefore mistakes are not being made that may confuse him, is very helpful at speeding along his learning process. When the dog is demonstrated for the owner and the owner gets a chance to work with him, it is much easier on both the owner and the dog to work together well due to the fact that the dog already knows what is expected of him. In addition, the owner's responsibility is cut down to working with the dog for half of the period of time each day (20 minutes), and the process can be completed on the owner's part in just two to three weeks. This time frame is much more practical for most owners in today's world. Our program provides an in-home lesson in this process as well, so that problems that occur in the home can also be dealt with.

This type of training is the most expensive type simply because the trainer is doing everything humanly possible to facilitate the training of the dog. In addition, all of the advantages to each type of training are available to the client. The caveat to this type of training is the necessity to find just the right facility to entrust with your dog. It is always a good idea to check references, see the facility, and watch the staff training prior to making your decision.

Equipment

For basic obedience training you will need the following equipment:

6 foot leather or nylon leash.

The type of leash is a personal preference, but it should be six feet long in order to allow you to get far enough away from the dog to practice the "stay" command. The width of the leash is typically ¾ inch, but can be smaller for a small dog or wider for an extra large dog. Leather is easier on your hands but nylon is harder for the puppy to chew.

30 foot long line.

The 30 foot long line is generally nylon and ½ inch wide. They do come in leather, but these are much more difficult to find and much more expensive. The thirty foot long line allows you to work the dog at a distance and teaches him that he must come when he's called, even if you are not near him.

Tab

A tab is a short piece of leash that hangs from the dog's collar so that you can easily grab it to make a correction. In the basic obedience portion of your course you will only use it while practicing the "place" command.

Training Collar

The typical collar used with the puppy in basic obedience will be a small-link, stainless steel, choke-style collar. There are exceptions to this style of collar that will be based upon the physical makeup of the puppy and its disposition. For dogs with weak necks and soft temperaments you may need to stay with a flat collar. For dogs with thick-muscled necks and strong dispositions you may need a pinch collar. Making this decision is critical to your success, but it should be done with professional assistance, due to the fact that the wrong collar can cause physical harm to the dog.

There are many misconceptions about training collars. People are confused about how to use training collars, and some are misinformed and believe that they are cruel devices. The truth is that a training collar is not cruel unless it is misused. This is the reason for being careful in deciding which collar to use. The choke chain is not in fact used to choke the dog when it is used properly. The dog should be able to be corrected, and the collar immediately released if it is being used properly. The dog should learn that, when he pulls on the collar, your reaction will be a quick jerk back and then a release when he is in the proper position. After a few lessons with you doing this, the dog learns to walk properly as it keeps the collar loose. When a dog is heavily muscled and tough (such as sometimes happens with Pit Bulls) the typical jerk and release on the training collar may not be enough. In this case a Pinch (prong) collar might be in order. This collar pinches the dog's skin when he pulls, and the jerk and release is more effective with this collar on a heavily-muscled dog. The opposite of this is the small breed, fine-necked breeds such as the Yorkshire Terrier or Chihuahua.

Some of these breeds may require a flat collar for training and just a slight jerk for a correction so as not to damage a delicate trachea.

Obedience Commands
Heel
Teaching "heel" will be much easier if the dog is already leash broken. Start with the dog on your left

The heel traditional heel position is on the left side with the shoulder next to your knee. The leash is held across your body with the left hand able to give the dog the appropriate signal or correction.

side and hold the leash across your body in your right hand. Your left hand should be loosely holding the leash over the top with your knuckles facing up. Start by patting your left leg with your left hand while stepping off with your left foot. Command the dog "Baron, Heel." Begin to encourage him with "Good Heel" the minute he comes along. If he pulls or balks, give him a quick jerk as a correction with a "No." Keep walking and encouraging him.

Make about-turns to maintain attention and pat your leg every time you turn, encouraging the dog to keep up with you. When you stop, if he continues, give him a jerk to get him to stop, command him to "sit" while you pull up with the leash and the first few times you may push down on his rear, rolling it backwards into a sit. Praise him whenever he assumes the position that you desire. After a few times showing him what you want, you will want to eliminate touching him, as he will become reliant on it. Always walk and stop quickly as it helps to keep the dog's attention from wandering.

If your dog's head is not up and its eyes are not looking at you, the problem will most likely be that you did not use your food and toy reward properly when he was a puppy. You should always intermittently reward

The sit command is accomplished with the right hand pointing at the dogs rear and the left hand positioned to control the dog or give a correction if needed.

your dog with either the food or the toy so that he has a reward to look forward to. When the dog is learning, you should be constantly talking to him and telling him whether he is doing well or not. The absence of this reinforcement results in a silence that causes the dog to question himself. Only as your dog gets very comfortable with the routine can your silent periods grow longer.

Sit

There are three different versions of the sit command that the dog needs to know:

Step 1

    Sit when told to (from any position)
    Sit in front (when called to come) Recall
    Automatic sit in the heel position

Using the food reward method detailed in Chapter V, continue in the same manner, but now substitute a toy as a reward. Show the puppy that the faster he sits, the faster he will get the toy or a rewarding game of fetch or tug. After you feel you have his full concentration, you can move on to polishing his performance.

Step 2

Adding corrections to your routine, you can cause the dog to understand that there is a slight consequence to a decision on his part not to do as you ask. By now, your dog should know to plant his rear on the ground when you command "sit." The next step you will add is to give him a "No" and jerk on the collar if he doesn't sit right away. When he comes to you on the recall, stops next to you on the heel, or is simply commanded to sit, his rear should hit the ground within a couple of seconds. Make sure that when he completes this task he is praised and rewarded immediately. When he hesitates or refuses to complete the command, his punishment will be your admonishment with "No" and a jerk, as well as your lack of praise and reward.

The left hand closest to the dog is used to give the down command so that the dog does not cross over in front of the handler.

Step 3

Now that the command is understood and the dog knows that you will give corrections when it is not completed, you can begin to speak to him less and move the reward to being intermittent. You want the possibility of reward to always be in his mind, but you do not want him to rely on it. By now your relationship should be such that the puppy will happily work for praise and look forward to the possibility of a special reward.

Down

The "Down" command tends to be the most difficult of all because in the dog's mind it is a submissive command. *The older the dog is when you begin to teach this command, the harder it will be to teach.* This is especially true with the dominant working breeds. You will be much further ahead if you have begun to teach the concept of down to the pre-school puppy. If you have not done this yet, refer to the food reward process in Chapter V.

When you progress to a toy, as with the other commands, you will want to give the puppy the toy when it lies down rather than throwing the toy or playing with the pup. If you were to play with the puppy at this point, it would negate the training for the "down" command as the puppy will forget the reason that it received the toy. Giving the puppy the toy when it lies down will promote the command in that it will play into the possessiveness of the puppy without activating its play drive.

Depending on the nature of your dog, the presence of the toy may allow the pup to stay in the down position longer. If the opposite proves to be true with your pup and he begins to play with the toy and scoots across the ground, you may need to eliminate the toy and only use food and praise as the reward.

The stay command is given with the palm toward the dog while the left hand holds the leash in case a correction is needed.

When the dog is on the stay command the handler can patrol in a circle around the dog so that the dog is conditioned to stay in one place even as the handler moves.

Stay

The "Stay" command was not used with the preschool puppy because of the lack of attention span. Even though the puppy has matured to the point of being able to learn the stay command, we still need to realize that four to six months of age is not mature enough to hold this position for a prolonged period of time. We need to ensure short-term success now in order to build up to longer periods in the future.

Start with the pup at the "Heel" position. Give the desired command to sit or down. Do not use the toy or food on this command, as our puppy will be motivated to come toward you. Signal a "Stay," holding the palm of your left hand firmly in front of the dogs' nose.

1. Step out in front of the dog using your right foot to step off (about two to three feet), facing the dog.
2. Begin to walk slowly in a half circle around your dog, using your right foot always first as an added cue that he should stay.
3. Use soothing praise and frequently show the hand signal with your palm toward the dog like a stop sign.

Be on the alert for the dog to move toward you. Your body should be side view to the dog so that you are ready to step in lifting the leash upward to correct the dog. This should be done with quick timing, as this is important to cementing the dog's understanding of what he is being corrected for.

Sit/Stay
1. Correct in an upward manner for the sit/stay. Quickly place your pup back in the spot where he was before.

2. Give him the signal to stay with your palm up and toward him again. Praise him as he holds the position, while you begin your half-circle patrol around him again.

Down/Stay

1. While practicing the down stay, step in and step on the leash as the dog is getting up. This will anchor the dog to the spot.

2. Reach for the leash above where it is anchored. Correct the dog in a downward manner.

Once the dog is down, give the signal to stay by showing the palm of your hand. Step back out and begin to patrol in a half-circle again.

Anchoring the Dog

If you have a particularly difficult time with the dog moving toward you on the stay, you may want to "anchor" for a while until the dog gets the idea. You can anchor the dog using a tree or post.

Using a 30 foot long line, wrap it around the post or tree and connect the other end to your dog's collar. The line should go around the post at the same level the collar is on the dog. Thus, if this is used on the sit/

stay, the line will be between two to three feet from the ground.

On the Down/Stay, the line will be under the dog at ground level. To the dog, you will seem to be controlling the leash. If the dog tries to move toward you, it will be impossible. Your dog will be automatically corrected with any momentum he uses when trying to move toward you.

Come

The Recall or Come command should be introduced during free movement. Do not call a dog from a Stay

When the dog is called to come the handler backs away to give the dog more momentum.

position at this point. If this mistake is made, it will take much longer to teach the dog not to break the Stay.

We want to emphasize the Come command. This is because it is a key to protecting yourself from excessive liability as well as assuring your dog's safety. The food and toy rewards work well on this command because it encourages the dog to come to you quickly.

In competition of the AKC or Schutzhund variety, the dog must come front and sit, and upon command proceed to the heel position to finish the exercise.

In French and Dutch sports, the dog immediately proceeds to the Heel position. This is the way we prefer to train dogs if they are not going to compete in sports or competitions that require the aforementioned sit in front. Beyond this difference, the command is basically taught in the same fashion.

1. The dog is free wandering and sniffing around, not on any command. The release word "Okay" should have been given so that the dog knows it is not under command.

2. If you have been using food in the puppy stage, your dog will already associate coming to you with reward. If not, begin with the use of food. Call the dog to come and wave the food or toy.

3. As your dog comes to you, in order to have the dog sit properly, do the following: Sit in front—hold the toy (or food) in front of you. Say "Sit" and after he has been sitting for five or six seconds, give the toy or food reward and praise. Sit at Heel—As the dog comes to you, step back and bring the toy or food around behind you, right in front of his nose, with the dog following the toy behind your back. Bring the toy up over his head as he comes into the Heel position and say "Sit." Wait five to six seconds and give the toy and praise!

After your dog has learned to follow the toy, you can move on to the next step, keeping the toy on you (in your belt or pocket). Call the dog to you and into the proper sit position. If the dog does not follow through, use a leash correction. Once the dog has complied, give the toy and praise.

Be sure you are patient and do not go too quickly through these steps. Depending on the age of the dog you are training, each step can span a period of days or weeks.

Pairing Exercises

Training will go much smoother if you pair up exercises that complement one another. For example, the first lesson taught could be walking at the Heel Position and Come when called. They derive from the same concept: staying near the handler and sitting automatically.

Sit and Down are easier to teach when paired together, because the dog is in a stationary position when taught these commands. If you mix up movement commands and stationary commands, it is much more difficult for the dog to remember whether he is supposed to be stationary or moving.

To further give the dog momentum after the basics are mastered on the six foot leash, we begin to work the same commands on the thirty foot long line.

30 Foot Long Line Work

After the five basic obedience commands have been covered and you are happy with the dog's performance on the six-foot leash, you are ready to proceed to the long line. The long line is used to establish your control at a distance, while at the same time allowing the dog more freedom.

You will use the long line to begin to train your dog to understand that he needs to respond to you at a distance. Practicing with this device will help you to bridge the gap between on and off leash in the dog's mind. Your goal will be to make the long line as insignificant as possible in the dog's eyes. In reality, it is a very significant piece of equipment to you, as it allows you to control the dog's actions at a distance.

Heel

Begin by putting the bulk of the line in your right hand. This is away from the dog's line of vision as he sits on your left side. Drop the line behind your back and over your right shoulder. Now it will be out of sight, because it is coming to the dog's collar from behind him.

To simulate heeling the dog off leash we drop the long line off of the left shoulder so that while walking the line is behind the dogs line of vision. The handler can easily reach back to the line and correct the dog if necessary.

Keep your left hand swinging naturally as you do your heeling exercise, and make turns often. Try to use only your voice for correction and encouragement. If he gets way out of line, reach back to the line and give a quick jerk. Show the dog, if need be, that you still have the ability to correct him.

Turns

Practice a lot of squared turns to the left and right using this process. If the dog tends to lead, make more frequent left and about-turns in order to check his pace. If necessary, jerk just a little on the collar as you make the Turn in order to keep him alert and paying attention rather than forging ahead.

The slow dog will need about turns and right turns to learn to keep up. Instead of applying corrections into the turn, you will apply motivation and encouragement as correction will just cause him to lag more.

Come

Now the Recall command will involve more distractions than it did on the six foot leash. At this point, the dog should know what to expect when you call him. He now needs to come to you even if something else has his attention or someone is talking to him or tempting him with a toy or food.

Step 1

Call the dog away from someone who has his attention while he is standing freely on the long line. Give him a chance to respond and praise him immediately if he turns away from the person or object of interest. If he doesn't come away after a couple of seconds give him a sharp jerk on the line with a "No" and call him again. Praise him as he comes to you and direct him to the Heel position. Praise him again only after he sits at your side.

Step 2

During this step, you will want to make sure that the line is not so obvious as it was when you were forced to have it ready to make a correction. To do this, you must leave the line on the ground and call the dog using only your voice for encouragement and correction. If you need the line for correction, then you are not ready for this step. If the dog usually comes to you but makes a mistake only now and again, you can pick up the line from the ground and make the correction.

Step 3

Before you use this step be sure to have practiced the Sit and Down/Stay commands on the long line for at least 90 days prior to this step. This is very important as the Stay command must be solid prior to calling the dog from the Stay position, or you will be working against yourself.

Put the dog on a Sit/Stay and move to the end of the line. Call the dog to come after about a minute. Give a gentle tug on the line if the dog seems confused and encourage him when he gets up to come to you.

From here, finish your exercise with praise and reward. The Recall from the Down/Stay should be handled in the same manner. We suggest that you do the Recall from Down/Stay after the Recall from the Sit/Stay, as it is easier to pull a dog from a Sit position than from a Down.

Sit and Down Stay

With the help of the long line you can begin to teach your dog to Stay in either the Sit or Down position at a distance. You will want to work your way out to the end of the line slowly. If you hold the line as you did with the six foot leash, then the dog will probably move toward you because of the weight of the line. Instead of doing this, put the line on the ground and make sure that you can step on it if the dog attempts to run out of position. You should wait until your dog can easily stay in place with you thirty feet away before you add distractions.

Distractions

Distractions are very important at this juncture in training. Do not go crazy throwing everything you can think of at the dog. Work your way through the process, slowly giving him one step at a time. Always be ready to correct when providing a distraction. Make sure that your corrections are swift and to the point. If your timing is too slow, the correction will lose its meaning. Possible distractions include:

1. Other dogs working in the same area.
2. Other people milling about in the area.
3. People talking to him (not with commands).
4. Loud noises such as dropping boards or pounding nails, gunshots, etc.
5. Throwing balls, oranges, rocks, sticks, etc.
6. Food thrown near him.
7. Cats, rabbits, squirrels, livestock, etc.
8. Road noise such as cars, trucks, and motorcycles.

VII. MANNERS AND PROBLEM SOLVING

Problem solving and home manners take on a more important role once the puppy hits four months of age. You have now seen him through the critical fear and socialization periods, and you will notice that at about four months of age he will tend to push your buttons more and become more defiant. It's what we call the "terrible twos" of puppyhood. This type of behavior also serves as a signal to you that he is ready to learn elementary-level training, as well as the home manners that you will expect from him for the rest of his life.

Home Manners

Home manners are defined as the limits that you set for the puppy in your home environment. There are three different home manners that we teach as a standard for behavior in and around the home:

Boundary Control: Teaching the puppy to stay within set boundary limits in the house or yard. Teaching the puppy not to go into the street unless released by a word such as "Okay" for safety reasons.

Door Crashing: Another safety rule that teaches the pup not to dash out doors or gates and to wait until he hears the release such as "Okay" prior to coming in or out.

Place Command: Teaching the puppy to come into the house and lie down in a specific place in the house that you designate for him. This is usually a bed, blanket, or rug in an area that is convenient for you.

Boundary Control

First, you will need to decide where you want your boundaries to be. In most homes, we recommend starting with curbs leading into the street. Next we work on areas that lead into other people's properties. Many times these areas are not well marked. You may want

Boundary Control is accomplished with a 30 foot long line teaching the dog that it must stay within the boundaries through a combination of corrections, praise, and setting the dog up to make a mistake through distraction until staying in the yard is well established in the dogs mind.

to use an object to mark this area temporarily for the dog. If there is a sidewalk involved, you can use a garden hose or a small board to mark the spot. After the puppy gets used to the general area, you can remove the object. On property that is more rural, you may use a rope strung between trees at the dog's eye level. In a small area such as an apartment or a condominium complex, the owner may want to have the puppy stop before getting to sidewalks or pathways.

The rule of thumb is that the boundary control is to be used for safety purposes and not as an absolute.

Even if the puppy has been respecting his boundaries for months while you are present, you still should not leave him alone and expect the same from him. You should think of this in the same way as you would with a three-year old. You teach him not to run into the street, but you don't expect that you can go in the house and leave him outside alone by a busy street.

You always want to start to establish the manners after the basic obedience has been taught. This is because it is less confusing due to the fact that you have already established basic communication with the dog. You will have taught him the down stay, which makes it much easier to teach the "Place," which is basically a relaxed Down/Stay in a certain location. You will also have taught the puppy to walk on the leash properly, so that when you begin to tell him to stop at certain locations he won't be confused.

Step 1

Start with your puppy on the six foot leash and walk him along the boundary that you have chosen. If this is a curb, for instance, you will want to walk him along the entire curb, being careful that he doesn't step into the street. Next, bring the puppy slowly toward the street, but as you step into the street pull up on the leash and bring the dog backwards telling him "No." When he stops at the curb be sure to praise him. You must be sure to correct him quickly to make the association. If he manages to step into the street, pull him out quickly, as if the street was dangerous and he needed to get out of it quickly. Circle back into the yard and try stepping into the street from a different location. Repeat the correction and praise as it is justified. If he stops on his own, make sure to praise him immediately and strongly.

Step 2

After your puppy is stopping consistently at the curbs where he must step down, try working with him on the driveway, where there is not such an obvious boundary. This may take a period of time for him to understand, because dogs do not see details as well as we do. Repetition is your key to success when practicing boundary control. Once he is doing this well on all boundary areas, you may add in distractions such as changing your pace or distracting him by bouncing a ball.

Step 3

Once you have established the boundaries well on the six-foot leash, it is time to work with them on the thirty-foot long line. Don't make the mistake of assuming that the pup will do well just because he did so on the six-foot leash. Moving a distance away from you can give the puppy the false impression that you don't have control. In addition to using the distance as a distraction, you can add whistling, having someone else talk to him, and tossing around a toy. The one thing you want to avoid is using his name and words like "Come On" or anything that would sound like a command.

Release Word "Okay"

It is very important not to release the dog into the street until you have firmly established that the street is a forbidden zone. This is different from Door Crashing, in that where Door Crashing is concerned you must release him through the doors by necessity. Since you obviously need to walk in and out of doors on a daily basis, you cannot take as long to teach him the release command and, in fact, you must do this from the time that you begin teaching the dog. Where boundary control is concerned, it is paramount that you don't begin releasing him right away, because you do not have to walk the puppy in the street and you can certainly wait three weeks or more to take him on a walk that involves taking him in the street.

Door Crashing

The term "Door Crashing" can be misleading. Door Crashing involves teaching the dog not to run out of, or rush into, doors or gates. We will handle this in an almost identical manner as Boundary Control, with the single exception that we begin to release the dog through the door immediately and we make him stop in both directions.

We teach the dog to stop at doors and gates so that he won't dash out the door when he sees us opening it, and to keep him from knocking us over as he rushes through the door. In addition, door crashing is

Stopping at doors and gates without a command should be started in conjunction with basic obedience. The dog does not have to sit as long as it stops when it sees a threshold.

an excellent means to help establish and retain our dominance in the dog's mind. Dominant dogs have a habit of running through doors ahead of their owners. You are establishing your leadership when you make the dog wait for you to walk through a door or gate before he is allowed to.

Step 1

Door Crashing is simple to teach, but requires 100% consistency and repetition in order to properly instill the habit. If you are inconsistent, then the puppy will learn to test you to see if he can slip by without your noticing. The method is rather simple. Bring the puppy to the doorway on the six-foot leash. Walk through the doorway first. If he tries to go through, give him a quick jerk backwards and correct with a verbal "No." Praise him as soon as he stops and waits. He does not have to assume any particular position, because we are trying to simulate how he will act if he is not under any command when the door is opened. If you had to give him a command to stop (or required him to assume a certain position), the effect would be lost if you weren't present when the door was opened. After making him wait for you, you should then release him through the door with "Okay" and then praise him as he comes through the door. Practice this in both directions.

Step 2

After you have the puppy conditioned to wait until you walk through the door before he is released, you can begin something more difficult. Use distractions, such as strangers, toys, whistling, etc. to ensure that the puppy will be able to maintain his vigilance even under distraction. The puppy will soon learn that you are playing a game to see if you can trick him into moving. This actually works to teach him to make up his own mind and not be fooled into making a mistake.

Step 3

Let the puppy drag the long line in the house until he seems to have forgotten that he has it on. Have someone go out the front door and leave it open. Be ready, so that if the puppy makes a dash for the door you can step on the long line and stop him in his tracks. Give him a good correction for breaking his house rules and set him up repeatedly until he will not leave, even if the door is standing open for several minutes at a time.

Place Command

The place command will allow you to spend much more time with your dog. Having the dog come in and lie down in a spot that you have designated

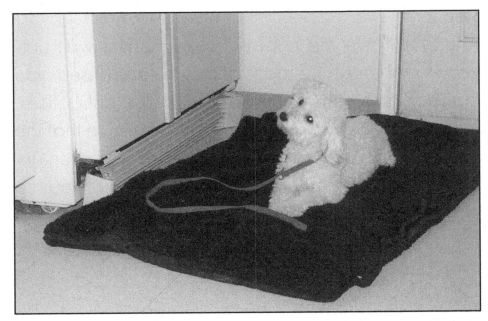

A bed, blanket, or rug can be established in various rooms of the house in order for the dog to remain in one place. This makes it easier to clean up hair or dirt, and to have company over without the dog jumping on them.

for him allows you to have him with you even if you need to be engaged in activities such as cooking, cleaning, watching television, or surfing the internet. In addition, the place command helps you keep a clean house, since any dirt and hair that is left by the dog will all be located in the place you have designated him to lie.

The place command is best taught after the puppy is used to coming into the house in the crate and after he knows the Down/Stay command. This way, you won't be trying to get him used to something that he hasn't previously been exposed to.

Step 1

Bring the puppy in the house on the six-foot leash. After you release him through the door with "Okay," point him towards the "Place" you want him to learn as his own and give him the command "Place" in an enthusiastic voice. Continue to say "Place" as you lead him to his bed. When you get to the designated spot, point in the same manner as you would on the Down command and give him the Stay hand signal, but all while saying "Place." You can help the puppy to understand what you expect of him the first few times if it seems necessary, but you should stop giving the extra commands as soon as possible. Make sure that you stay in the room with the puppy so that you can correct him if he attempts to get up. Use the three strikes rule on the dog throughout this process. If he gets up, correct him the first couple of times, but on the third time he attempts to get up put him outside. As a form of punishment you want him to be in a place that he cannot see you or be with you for at least twenty minutes before you attempt the "Place" command again. Start by expecting the "Place" command to be maintained for only 15–20 minutes at a time. Of course, if your puppy falls asleep or stays quiet, you can keep him there longer. Your goal will be to work your way up to two hours at a time.

Step 2

Bring the puppy in the house, point towards his "place" and expect him to begin to walk by himself to this point. You should see him beginning to lie down automatically, without any direction from you. Of course, if he needs some assistance in getting there or being reminded to lie down, you should do so. If this is the case, it will be an indication that you haven't really left step one yet. You can make the place command more attractive by giving him something to chew on once he assumes the position. This can be a favorite toy or a new treat, depending on how the puppy acts when he has them. Remember that the "Place" will be more satisfying to the puppy if it is warm in the winter and cool in the summer. Comfort is very important to the puppy and will go a long way toward making the puppy willing to go to the "Place."

Step 3

Now that the puppy is going to the "Place" virtually on his own, you will want to begin using the Tab (short leash or handle) attached to his collar, rather than the leash. At this point you will only need to grab the Tab and correct him when necessary. This is the precursor to your off-leash training in the home. It is very important that you always have some sort of leash, even a short one to enable you to make a correction. At this point, the conditioning should be well established, and you should be making very few corrections.

Problem Solving

The most common reason that people seek out a professional dog trainer is to solve existing problems. Using K-9 Companions' system of Confinement Conditioning and Instinctual Corrections, you should be able to prevent many of these problems before they develop into habits.

Housebreaking

Housebreaking begins as soon as you purchase the puppy. The most effective way to go about housebreaking the dog is prevention. You must adhere to a routine for elimination that the puppy can count on. As a rule of thumb, the puppy should be put out every two hours, after each meal, and after waking (in the morning or following naps). The puppy should be monitored carefully when not in the crate.

Newspaper or Wee Wee pads should be avoided on the floors, as they will only serve to confuse the puppy. If you are away and cannot monitor the puppy during the day, a puppy pen with wood shavings should be supplied, and it should be located in a neutral environment such as a basement, garage, or outdoors, dependant on weather conditions.

Doggy Door Method

In apartments, condominiums, or many homes a doggy door could be the ultimate solution to a housebreaking problem. Most people with large breeds choose not to use this method, as the passage way for the dog has to be large enough that a small person or child might be able to intrude by using it. For small dogs, however, this is not a factor. You should anticipate some inconvenience if you choose to use this method, as you will need to place a crate in front of the doggy door. This inconvenience can be minimized or eliminated altogether if you are able to utilize a door that is not normally used by your family, or you choose to place the doggy door in the wall of a room that is out of the path of foot traffic. The inconvenience is caused by the fact that the wire crate needs to be placed up against the doggy door temporarily in order for this method to work properly. For some people the idea of the dog being able to come in out of the elements but not into the rest of the house (unless desired) is so tempting that they will want to make this a permanent situation.

Step 1

The doggy door will be installed in a door or wall, where it will lead out to a protected run area where the dog can potty and have fresh water and food (at feeding times). The area should afford both shade and shelter, and a cover should be provided if the dog is small and there are predators in the area. A wire crate should be utilized in the house. This type of crate can be modified by removing the back or utilizing a pre-cut door, or by using wire cutters to modify a door on the side or back. This allows you to have a door opening toward the house, as well as one out of the doggy door. The puppy's blanket (or bed) and toys should be allowed inside. You may need to tape the doggy door open for a few days until the puppy is comfortable enough with the situation to push it open himself. The puppy will not want to soil his bed, so he will jump out of the door to exercise, eat, and drink. (This step should be used for dogs up to puberty or for a minimum of three months for conditioning in an older dog.)

Step 2

The next step is to give the puppy just enough room inside the doggy door so that he has to go a little further to make an effort to go out and potty. An exercise pen (there are many on the market made of metal or plastic) can be placed just inside the door. The puppy's bed and toys again are inside, but there is three to four times the space inside for the puppy. You will want to be sure that the flooring is non-absorbent in order to prevent the puppy from having accidents. If you must put the doggy door in the area where there is carpet, consider putting down plastic carpet runners temporarily to keep the puppy from urinating on or chewing the carpet. (This step applies to the puppy from nine to sixteen months.)

Step 3

Your next step is to give the dog the entire room to come in and out of the house, using the doggy door and a baby gate barrier to the rest of the house. At any time you can go back a step or utilize more confinement when you are not home and less when you are. You should also utilize the place command in the rooms that you are in so that you can keep track of the dog's activities. (This step applies from sixteen to twenty-four months.)

Step 4

The final step is giving the dog the entire house. By this time he should be mature, and he should have proven to you that he is trustworthy. You may still have to take one step back from time to time in order to be sure that you are comfortable giving him the entire house while you are away. (This step applies beyond twenty-four months.) It should be mentioned that if you can achieve any of these steps prior to the age brackets associated with them, you should feel free to go on to the next step. These age frames are simply averages based on typical maturity and average client conditioning.

Crate Training Method

This is the preferred method for large dogs, simply because of their size. We prefer to teach the pup to come in and lie down in one spot in conjunction with the crate training method. In this way you can have the dog lying in a relaxed "down/stay" for part of the time you are home, and in the crate for the portion of the time when you cannot be observing him. You will not be able to start the "Place" command however, until the puppy is obedience trained, so you will start with using the crate whenever you cannot be directly with him.

Step 1

When beginning this method, the puppy must be eight weeks old or older. Start by bringing the puppy into the house for no more than two hours at a time, using the crate with a blanket inside to make it comfortable. The puppy should have a safe, non-ingestible toy in the crate. This is also a good time to give him a special treat that he doesn't have the opportunity to get anywhere else. After the appropriate amount of time, take the puppy outside to exercise and go to the bathroom. If you see that the puppy is sleeping, you can wait until he wakes up before you take him out. If the puppy cries to get out, you may want to put him in another room so that you don't have to listen to him. You don't want to make the mistake of letting him out every time he cries. The puppy should only be free in the house if you are directly with him and watching his every move.

Step 2

You should not expect the puppy to stay in the crate for the entire night without an accident until he is over four months of age. Make sure that the crate is small enough that he can't go to the bathroom and move away from the mess. If this happens, he may not get used to holding it all night because he has the room to go in the crate. You may have to get up in the middle of the night for a time longer to let a young puppy out. The amount of time that it takes to be able to make it through the entire night will vary from puppy to puppy. The rule of thumb should be that you should accomplish this no later than when he is five months old and done with his teething process, which can produce temporary set backs.

Step 3

After he finishes his basic obedience commands and knows how to maintain the Down/Stay command, you are ready to use the "Place" command when you are in the room, and to use the crate only when you are too busy to watch him. Using the "Place" command will keep the dog from freely wandering around the house and going potty when you can't see him. These mistakes are self-rewarding and will lead to on-going problems, so you must avoid so much as letting this cycle start. Make sure that you let the dog out to potty and exercise every two hours unless he is napping.

Corrections in Housebreaking

Confinement Conditioning eliminates ninety percent of your need to make a correction. Mistakes will still occur, usually due to owner error. When they happen, you need to show the pup that you are not pleased with his actions, but at the same time you need to **KEEP YOUR COOL!**

If you happen to witness a mistake, your immediate response should be to startle the dog. Yell a sharp "No" and clap your hands. If you have a squirt bottle, you can squirt the puppy in the nose to startle him. Put the puppy's nose down near the mess, but not in it and admonish him with the word "No." Next, take him to the area he should have gone to for elimination. Quickly pick up the mess with a paper towel (soak up urine) and take it to the correct area. Show the puppy and praise him.

Make sure that you completely clean the area with odor-masking cleaners made specifically for pet messes. Keep your puppy from returning to this area in the immediate future, as you do not want him to return to this area due to the smell and begin a negative cycle.

Chewing
All puppies relish chewing, as it is a natural process during teething. This is the way the puppy explores his world, due to the fact that he doesn't have hands to use. You should try to provide safe things for your puppy to chew on such as English Rubber Balls, Kong Toys, and non-destructible flavored bones. We would recommend avoiding things that swell once

A dog given freedom of the house can be very destructive in a short period of time.

they are wet in the dog's mouth (such as raw hide bones), since they have been known to have been the cause of many intestinal surgeries due to blockages. Anything that can be ingested will carry a certain amount of risk.

Unfortunately, items that can be destroyed are what the dog tends to enjoy most. For this reason, a good choice can be the large, store-bought bones that are meant to be eaten, or the pre-boiled shank and knuckle bones that are sterilized and sold wrapped in the stores. These can still be ingested, but do not swell in the dog's intestines. You should always supervise your dog as much as possible when he is chewing on something that can be ingested. If you cannot be there to observe your dog, it is best to leave him with only the safest toys.

Corrections for Chewing

Since chewing is natural to the dog and is not "wrong" (a human concept), it will be important to make an association for him about what is rewarding to chew on and what is not. When a dog learns that a certain object in his mouth results in a negative (smell, taste, or sound) association, he will learn to avoid these objects on his own.

Since the dog is set up by his very nature to explore with his mouth and discover what is rewarding and what is not, we can use that to our advantage in training. We call these kinds of corrections *instinctual corrections*. If, for instance, a dog chases a skunk, the resulting spray from the skunk can dissuade him from repeating the action. In much the same way, we can use a negative taste, smell, or sound association with chewing.

One of the easiest corrections to apply to the puppy is a spray of vinegar and water to the nose. The bottle should be set on stream and the aim should be for the nose. This should always be coupled with the word "No." Just as when he was a puppy under four months old, there are times when simply taking the puppy away from an area where he can chew is the most efficient thing to do. At some point after he is four months old, however, he is going to get a little more defiant and insist on having things that he shouldn't. This is the time to use these methods.

"Glop" is a mixture of hot Cayenne pepper and dish soap. You will want to mix this up and have it handy in the refrigerator. When the puppy chews on things that he shouldn't (such as your patio furniture or electrical cords), you should quickly cover them in the glop and take him to the offending article, making sure that he touches it with his mouth. The typical response will be to pull away, shake his head, or get a drink of water. Within five minutes the puppy will usually go back to explore whether or not that object still tastes offensive.

In most outdoor situations, you can leave the glop and let it dry. It is easily washed off because the base is soap, but you will want the puppy to realize over the course of several observations that the object is not pleasurable to chew on. Make sure that you always give him something afterwards, which does smell and taste good so that he can make the connection that some things work better than others when it comes to his choices.

Shake cans can be used to startle the pup when he is chewing on something he shouldn't. You want to take a snapshot in the puppy's mind as to what he was doing when the noisy shake can fell from the sky. A shake can is simply an aluminum can with five pennies inside. A soda can rinsed out (so that the pennies won't stick) is perfect. Turn the twist tab to cover the opening or tape over the top of it so that the pennies don't fall out. We recommend that you keep a few of these stashed around the house for the times that you want to make an instant correction from a distance. You should always pick up the can immediately after throwing it and saying "No" so that the puppy does not begin to use it as a toy. If this happens it will lose effectiveness. *It is very important when you make a correction to always follow it with giving the puppy something he can chew on* and praising him!

Playful Biting and Jumping Up on People

While the puppy is under four months old, it is important to remember to solve most problems by not letting them occur in the first place. This is done by a combination of confinement when you cannot directly supervise the puppy, and conditioning when you can. If the young puppy tends to want to bite on your hands, you should simply give him something to chew on which is interesting enough to hold his attention. Don't let him run around chasing a toddler, as you can predict that the result of this is going to be playful biting and the toddler crying. It is very important to control where your puppy is in relationship to other animals, children, or objects that can hurt him in the first four months of his life. After this period of time, he will be ready to train and through obedience and correction he can learn what you expect of him.

*As with chewing, the first thing you will want to utilize is the spray bottle with vinegar and water on stream. When the puppy tries to jump on you or children, squirt him in the nose and tell him "No." Next, ask him to "Sit" and give him a reward and praise. By doing this you are teaching him that jumping up for attention does not work, but sitting in front of you for attention is rewarded.

Next you will want to utilize the shake cans you have strategically put around the house (see chewing). When he tries to jump on you, your children, or guests, shake the can in his face telling him "No" and again make him "Sit" before your guests pet him.

If you are outside on a warm day, you can do a similar exercise with a cup of water. Many times guests in your home may stand around with a drink of some sort in their hands. Thus this exercise will simulate a circumstance that your puppy may see many times in his life. If he tries to jump on you or your guests as you stand in the yard, simply toss the drink (water) in his face and say "No." Again, call him to you and ask him to sit. Praise him only in the sit position. This will help to teach him to avoid people with drinks in their hands and thus keep people from having drinks spilled on them due to the dog jumping up.

Digging in the Yard

A dog left with the freedom of the yard prior to being taught how to deal with the freedom can amuse himself with your possessions.

If you are following our procedures of Confinement Conditioning utilizing the Dog run, Crate, and Puppy Pen, your digging problems should be almost non-existent. The conditioning part of the training requires that you know how to make on-the- spot corrections when the puppy attempts to dig while you are observing.

The first thing you will want to do when you observe the puppy digging is to startle him. You want to take that snap-shot in his brain so that he will remember what he was up to when the "shake can" magically fell from the sky. You should always use the word "No" in conjunction with any correction.

Second, you will want to go retrieve your glop from the refrigerator and put it in the hole or the scratch area where he was digging. Just as with chewing, you will want to take him over to the hole and make sure his mouth touches the glop while telling him "No." Then provide some form of positive entertainment for him, such as playing with a toy.

You should know that recently upturned dirt (such as the kind that results after you have planted something in your yard) is very tempting to the puppy because of all of the fresh odors associated with it. For this reason, you should avoid letting the puppy into freshly planted areas for three days immediately following your planting unless you are overseeing his every move. It will take about three weeks for the soil to become less interesting to him. Likewise, be aware that rodents, such as gophers and rabbits, can cause a dog to dig in an attempt to catch them as prey. To successfully eliminate the digging, you must first eliminate the rodents. You will need to make sure that you do this in a safe manner, so as not to poison or hurt your puppy in the process.

Excessive Barking and Whining

Barking, whining, and howling are natural forms of communication for the dog. This is how he communicates with other canines. The dog will naturally attempt to try to communicate with you using these same methods. Whether or not the dog begins to use these techniques in excess will largely be based on how you react to them. If the dog learns that you respond to his vocalizations by feeding him, talking to him, letting him in or out, or even just showing up when you've left him alone, he will quickly learn that he can communicate his desires to you and see his will fulfilled. To a small degree, this communication can be useful, such as when he needs to communicate that he needs to go outside to relieve himself. The problem starts when this communication translates into manipulation. This is very common with spoiled dogs. There is a rule in dog training that the question the owner must always ask themselves is "Who is being responsive to whom?" If you are responding to the dog's desires, you are showing him that he is the "Alpha" (leader of the pack), whereas if he always responds to you, you are the Alpha. This means that you must distinguish at what point the dog goes from communicating to manipulating and then set the ground rules for his vocalizations. There are many ways for you to communicate to him that you do not appreciate this manipulation.

Negative Noise: A sharp sound in association with his barking along with the word "No" can go a long way toward teaching him that you disapprove of excessive barking. This can be accomplished by using the "shake can" thrown at a screen door if he is barking at you through it. Place a metal object such as a piece of roofing tin or metal trash can near his run and throw a rock at it to make a booming sound in conjunction with the word "No," or you may use an air horn to startle him.

Water: Depending on the size of the dog and the weather outside, you can use anything from the spray bottle with vinegar and water to a cup of cold water thrown in his face to an actual hose to drench him. You will find that if your reaction is consistently applied every time he barks, it may take you up to a dozen times to get through to the dog, but he will eventually learn that the only response to his incessant barking is a squirt in the face. From that point on, a simple "No" shouted out the window should do it.

You will want to make sure that the dog is not legitimately trying to convey something to you. You should get to understand his different tones, as a dog's barks vary according to subject. There is a definite difference between an intruder alert and a bark to get your attention. Dogs communicate through vocalizing, so you will always want to make sure that there isn't something wrong. They will bark if they are cold, hungry, thirsty, afraid, lonely, or want to play. It is up to you to make sure that the basic needs of the puppy are met before you begin correcting him for inappropriate barking. Another thing that you can do to simplify things for yourself and the puppy is to be sure that he is in a place where he is not constantly being frustrated by neighborhood children or animals. Some dogs bark because they are sitting behind a fence witnessing children playing or coming home from school. When you have a circumstance such as this, you will need to create a barrier to keep the dog from witnessing these events, or make sure that he is kept indoors at certain times of the day. You can often use a crate in an extra bedroom and turn on the television or radio to create covering noises so that the dog will not even realize that children are playing nearby.

Always remember while problem solving that the main causes for problems with dogs are *boredom, frustration, and jealousy*. If you can find a way to eliminate the root of the problem, you can generally solve the associated behaviors. In this way, raising a puppy is

A dog left alone to roam the house can easily check out the food on the table or counter in your absence.

similar to raising a child. It is, in fact, a good idea for a young couple to raise a puppy to adulthood prior to raising a child. This exercise will teach them where they differ philosophically in the rearing process. It will also show which of them is most likely to get up in the middle of the night to care for the puppy and to clean up messes or take charge of disciplinary matters. This can be a real eye opener. Regardless of what discipline measures you engage in, you should *never hit the puppy!* Yelling and screaming don't work either. Yelling only serves to let you blow off some steam.

Unfortunately, these actions will likely cause your dog to cower and submissively urinate. Your puppy will become insecure, as he perceives you as trying to show your dominance toward him, yet does not associate his action with your behavior. This is because canines do not have a concept of right and wrong. Why would they? There is no morality in the canine's world, only dominance and subordination. Do not let yourself become stressed out in the process of problem solving. Your key to success is consistency and repetition, as well as our method of **Confinement Conditioning.**

Give yourself and the dog two years to work your way to complete trust, to include freedom of the house and yard. If you look at this as a long-term project rather than a quick fix, you will find you have much more patience. If you use Confinement Conditioning in the process, you will have much less destruction to deal with along the way.

VIII. MIDDLE SCHOOL (9–12 MOS)

A dog 9–12 months of age is considered to be a teenager and ready to go on to a higher level of learning with the freedom of training off the leash.

All of us remember those awkward middle school years, when you're not quite a little child anymore but not really a teenager either. Dogs go through the same period at about nine to twelve months of age. This is generally when the male's hormones will start to flow, an era usually indicated by the beginning of his leg-lifting. The female will usually come in season at this time as well. These are times when it is not unusual to see the dog (who is likely as large as an adult) still acting like a puppy at times. This is also the time when your puppy sometimes surprises you with behaviors that you might consider to be more adult than in the past. Like a middle school adolescent, your dog is just growing up.

It is at this time that we choose to advance his training into off-leash obedience. Since this is the adolescent age for dogs, you are also more likely to see adolescent behavior at this time. He may act like an adult on some days and like a puppy on others. The aforementioned behavior is normal for this age group. Up until this point, your training should have been very positive, and your expectations should have been reasonable since you have been working with a puppy on elementary behaviors. It is time now to take your expectations up a notch. Your puppy's attention span has grown, as has his body, and he is now ready for a more disciplined approach.

You will now want to begin to correct your dog for behavior that is less than precise. If he sits too slow or lags on a turn, you can now be more demanding. At this age, we drop ninety percent of the food reward and leave ten percent for intermittent reward.

We can pull a toy out as a "jackpot" reward at the end of a particularly good exercise, but we want to rely mostly on praise. You will be part of a delicate balancing act at this point in his training, since you will want your correction to be strong enough to make an impression, but not so strong as to impair the dog's forward momentum.

Tone of Voice

By far, the greatest asset in training your dog is your tone of voice. Dogs naturally relate to each other in tones. Low growling tones are used to communicate displeasure or a threat. High-pitched whining noises are used for excited greetings and pleasure. Because the dog is naturally set up to receive messages through tones, this aids our ability to communicate with him. It is our vocal tones and the consistency with which we communicate through these tones that will ultimately train the dog well. It will be very important in off-leash training to have mastered these tones (along with the leash corrections) because with off-leash training you are primarily using your voice to control the dog.

Displeasure-"No"

By now you should have been practicing with your dog for at least three months, utilizing both the six and thirty foot leashes so that you are able to make a physical correction associated with the "No." If you have been consistent, you should now be able to correct the dog verbally and have him correct his own behavior. Because the concept of working off leash will be new for both of you, we will begin by using a light line (small breed leash), dragging on the ground or tucked into your left front pocket. This leash should be four to six feet in length, depending on the size of your dog. You want just enough leash to allow the end to be able to sit in your pocket or to be dragging so that you can step on it to make a correction. You can also make your own light line out of parachute cord and a small clasp. Your dog should be conditioned enough to your corrections that this light line provides enough control for you. If it does not, this will signal that you need to go back a step and practice more with the six and thirty foot heavier lines. This line will provide you with the ability to test the dog for its readiness to go off the leash. You will have this line only as a safety measure and to provide the needed correction if he tests you. It is very important at this point that your "No" is firm, quick, and precisely uttered at the time of the mistake.

Pleasure: "All Right" "Good Job" "That-a-Boy"!

High-pitched tones that express genuine pleasure will be all that most dogs need for motivation and focus.

It is very important that you are willing to dish out an abundance of praise as you work with your dog off-leash. As you begin to control the dog with your voice only, your goal is to keep him motivated and focused on you without having to utilize the leash to keep him in the proper place. A wagging tail, a high head, and a bounce in his step are all indications that you are doing a good job of keeping his attitude positive. Keeping the reward of a toy or food as a "jackpot" at the end of a good performance will always serve to help keep the dog's attention on you.

Physical praise (petting and hugging) should always be reserved for the end of a good performance, as they will tend to pull your dog's focus away from the job at hand. The dog will not be able to absorb commands if he is distracted by touch stimuli.

Commands-Neutral or Positive
Your commands should always be given as neutral (matter of fact) or positive ("good stay") rather than shouted at the dog or given in a dominant tone. Keep in mind that the dog is set up by nature to read your tone of voice. If the dog interprets the command as being demanding, his performance will be reserved, as he will anticipate a correction. In this way, the

dog's expectations become a self-fulfilling prophecy. He will be afraid to make a mistake and, by becoming self-conscious, he will make a mistake and be corrected for it. This will then teach the dog to fear the command, as it will be followed by a reprimand. If, on the other hand, the dog perceives you to be at least neutral (if not happy) about giving the command, he will anticipate the neutrality or praise associated with the tone of your command.

Light-Line Training

Prior to having the complete freedom off leash the light line (small breed leash) can be used to simulate off leash training while still allowing you the freedom to step on the leash to stop the dog if it should try to bolt.

As previously mentioned, the light-line is a safety net for you between the on and off leash training. Attach the light-line to the dog's training collar and proceed through your training as if you had a leash attached. Having the light line to grab or step on in order to correct your dog will give you the confidence to attempt to give the commands without the security of the six or thirty foot leashes, while at the same time giving the dog the additional freedom he needs to decide that he will in fact comply with your commands. It is at this time that the rough edges in his training and your control will become apparent. It is critical that you use your voice to constantly reinforce that he is either doing well or making mistakes. Your voice, as well as your willingness to give or withhold reward, will be the beacon by which your dog judges his own performance.

Follow the exact same steps that you did in the basic on leash obedience program, with the exception of starting on the light-line only at the six foot distance. If you go too far, too fast, he may take advantage of the knowledge that he is off of the leash and bolt. At this point, you will have to go back to the thirty foot long line because he will otherwise be teaching himself that he *does not* have to listen to you when he is not on a leash. This is most likely to happen with dogs that have played chase games with their owners. Chase games where the owner or a child chases the dog around the home or yard only serve to teach the dog to run away from the owner when they do not have the control of the leash. This pattern can be very hard to break due to the fact that the dog is being taught through the chase game *not to come to you when he is called.*

Grab-Tab

If the dog does well on the light line and does not need a reprimand in his performance, you can begin to use the grab-tab. This is no more than a hand hold on the end of a clasp. The grab-tab can be bought in a store or made. A cut off end of a leash that allows you 4–10 inches of leather or nylon at the end of the clasp will do. You will find tabs in the form of a loop (hand hold), flat, or braided piece, as long as it allows you to grab the handle to make a correction.

You do not want to move on to using only the tab in your obedience training until you have mastered the six foot leash, thirty foot leash, and light-line. Here, using your voice properly, and utilizing reward in the form of toy, food, or ultimate tactile praise is the ace up your sleeve. You must be careful not to dish out those rewards too frequently, as you will find yourself being the victim of your dog's blackmail if he begins to push your buttons by acting poorly until you pull out the rewards. You must be sure that you, not the dog, maintain control during this phase of the training.

Once the dog is working off leash the grab tab is used so that you have a handle to correct or lead the dog with should you need to. Trying to grab the collar without this device can result in broken or sprained fingers.

By now, you have been practicing obedience with your dog for three months or more, and at times you both have probably become bored with the inhibition of his freedom of movement that is part of the discipline. This is a good time to let your dog learn agilities as an outlet for his more playful side. Agilities can do that, as they teach the dog how to jump, climb, and balance, but you will need to make sure that you don't overdo it, as he still has growing bones and joints when he is not yet mature. Make sure that he is not allowed to launch himself off of high places or to jump on such a regular basis that he begins to be effected in his joints. At the same time, teaching him to do moderate jumps, climb ladders, and navigate cat walks will all be fun for him and provide a release of the tension that can be built up with inhibitive exercises.

It is important when you introduce the agilities that you do not force the dog into compliance. The introduction should be done in such a way that it is soothing and comfortable for the dog. When you first approach the agilities with the dog, all of your obedience mentality should be gone. You want to ease the dog into being comfortable with the idea of jumping, climbing, and balancing. This is a matter of confidence not obedience. Set the high jump low enough that both you and the dog can walk over it. As you approach the point where the dog has to jump, command "hup" in a positive voice. As soon as he makes it over the jump, lavish him with praise and a toy. Do this at the same height three times before making the jump slightly higher.

When using a vertical incline, you should climb it and sit at the top. The best set of circumstances is to have a spotter who can keep the dog from jumping off the opposite edge while you climb up. Once at the top, make the dog stop next to you and pet him in order to calm him down and let him realize that it is not scary to be at the top of the incline. Next, have the spotter lead him down the rest of the way without jumping. The dog should get used to climbing down rather than jumping off of the top of the incline. He should not get the food or toy reward until he reaches the bottom. You should praise him lavishly at this point.

With the cat walk, you should be careful that the dog does not jump off at any point, as there are many areas where the dog could do so. A spotter is necessary to teach the dog to stay on top and walk across the plank. If the cat walk starts with a resting station, it is a good idea to stop the dog here and make him "down." This allows him to collect himself after he has climbed to the top and to calm down. He should learn that he is only going to receive the reward after he has successfully crossed the cat walk and climbed down the other side. As with our earlier methods, practice this carefully at least three times prior to giving him any more leash or freedom without help from a spotter.

Stepping Up Your Searching, Tracking, & Retrieving

This is a good time in your dog's life to take his searching, tracking and retrieving skills to the next level. He is still not a mature adult, but he should be starting to be trustworthy while off of his leash. His attention span should be growing to the point that he can track a little longer (following human scent on the ground with his nose), search a little farther (using air scent), and retrieve at longer distances.

Tracking

After having given your dog tracking experience when he was young, you can begin to take him out to areas where you can track in actual vegetation such as an alfalfa field. You can now begin to do a basic track with your dog walking behind with a tracking line. After doing straight tracks, you can begin to make turns at right angles, using food every few feet and a large food or toy reward at the end. Since there is not enough room in this book to go into tracking in detail, please refer to one of the books on tracking in the suggested reading section of this book.

Searching

At this point in your dog's life, you can begin to run searches outdoors in much the same way that you practiced with him as a young puppy in the house. This is the time to make an outdoor game of "hide and go seek." This is fun for the dog and can begin to help him to search for hidden people using his nose. When the person is found, the dog should be given lavish praise and food or toy reward. Since we do not have enough room in this book for a complete guide to searching, please refer to books on searching in the suggested reading section of this book.

Retrieving

Up to this point, you should have been practicing retrieving as fun and games. Now you will want to formalize your retrieval training by making your dog stay at your side while you throw the ball (dumb bell, etc) and giving him a command to send him after the item. You will want to bring him in to sit in front of you using the 30 foot long line until he becomes reliable and used to the routine. Have him release the object by giving him an "out" command. And then ask him to return to the heel position. Many dogs are possessive of their ball and will not want to release it. A tidbit of food can be given upon successful release or another toy upon completion. The toy is usually the least effective, as many dogs will spit out the first toy before completion of the recall in anticipation of receiving the next one.

We find that the best reward for retrieving is usually a combination of food reward on release with the toss of the toy upon completion of the heel command. The retrieval should always be fun and accompanied by food and toy reward in the beginning in order to establish a routine. If there is compulsion associated with the retrieval, it will no longer be fun and rewarding for the dog, and this can result in a refusal to retrieve. Since there is not enough room to write an entire book on retrieving here, please refer to the Suggested Reading Section for books on retrieving training.

Proofing Your Off-Leash Training

Although moving to off-leash training is basically reviewing your six and thirty foot basics while moving on to the use of the light line and tab, you should still be aware that this is a big step for your dog. In addition to learning to work without benefit of a leash, you should be proofing him against distractions. While you are working off-leash in a safe and contained area, you will want to look for distractions for your dog. Strangers trying to call him, balls rolling past, Frisbees flying, startling banging sounds, and the presence of other dogs that can perform obedience near him will all be helpful if you plan to compete with your dog or take him places where control while off the leash is very important.

Although you are training the dog to work obedience off the leash, you will want to be cautious as to where and how you practice this. You do not want to put your dog in danger by practicing in places where there is traffic or other dangers. Even though dog parks seem like obvious places where working on off leash with distractions would be appropriate, the opposite is often true. The problem with dog parks is the people and dogs that come to them. A prime example is a client of ours who owned a sweet little Labrador puppy that was only five months old. She thought it would be fun and good socialization for her puppy to go to the dog park and have a chance to play with other dogs. After she had been at the park for fifteen minutes, a car pulled up and released two Pit Bulls off-leash that proceeded to attack her puppy. Her puppy had to be taken to the veterinarian for stitches, and he was never trusting of dogs he didn't know thereafter. Another factor to keep in mind is leash laws. In some states, if your dog does anything that causes harm in any way when he is off leash in public, you will automatically be 100% at fault. This means that if your dog caused a car to swerve and hit a tree, or caused an elderly person to fall down, or bit another person or animal, you would be strictly responsible because the dog was off leash.

IX. HIGH SCHOOL: ADVANCED OBEDIENCE (12–18 MONTHS)

Agility training helps to build confidence in the dog and is a fun outlet that is an offset to the inhibiting nature of obedience training.

This is a very important stage in your dog's life. It can also be a very trying time for you and your dog, much as it would be with any teenager. This is a transitional age for our dog, as this is the age of sexual maturity. Somewhere in this age range your bitch will come into season for the first time. The male dog's cue that he has reached sexual maturity will be when he starts to lift his leg to urinate.

As a result of this physiological change, mature dogs will become a little more serious and defense minded.

How you handle your relationship with your dog at this juncture of the training process is critical to your success.

Start to think of yourself more as a coach with this age group. Your desire should be to instill confidence and cheer your dog on to greater achievements. When you see the inevitable regression that will take place from time to time with a teenager, you should simply adjust your techniques in order to get your dog moving forward again.

Your Goals At This Time Should Be:
1. Strengthen the bond between you and your dog. You can do this through time spent and activities together, such as traveling and sports that you can share.
2. Make sure that your dog understands that you are in charge and that, even though he is a teenager and may want to be dominant with you or others, he is not going to be uncontrollably aggressive.
3. Add to your basic on and off leash Obedience with Advanced Obedience and Agility training that will strengthen your confidence and communication.
4. Give yourself an attitude check. Remember that although your dog is large in size, he is still young in the brain. The average age of maturity for

competition purposes is two to two and one half years. You cannot control how quickly your dog matures, but you can control the timing of your dog's training.

Advanced Obedience Exercises

Some of the obedience exercises that you can teach your dog will apply to your everyday needs and desires for travel and work. In addition, some of these exercises can be used in obedience or sport competitions. In any case, these exercises are a progression from basic obedience skills to more advance applications.

Sit & Down Stay with the Handler Out of Sight

At this point, your dog should be able to perform the Sit and Down Stay off leash, and for several minutes at a time. We will now work on the dog's ability to do this with you out of sight. Start with the long line stretched out thirty feet toward the blind (hidden area) that you are in. This way, if your dog moves, you will be able to catch the line immediately. At first, move into the blind for only thirty seconds. Increase the time (thirty seconds at a time) until you are doing this for several minutes.

Next, you can practice the same exercise with just the light leash until you never have to correct the dog. When you must correct, make sure you take the dog back to the exact starting point with a quick jerk to let him know that this will not be tolerated. Make sure that your corrections are timed properly. Make sure you say "No" just as soon as the dog breaks the stay. Since it will take you a few seconds to get to him and you do not want to do this in such a way that you startle him into bolting, your quick admonition is important at the exact second he makes the mistake.

Only when the dog is no longer making mistakes with the light line will you want to attempt to do this exercise utilizing the tab. When you put on the tab, you are essentially working the dog off leash. There is no difference to him when he is wearing the tab between being on or off leash. The difference for you is that you will have something to grab onto other than his collar if you need to make a correction. Many people have had their fingers strained or broken attempting to grab the ring on the training collar. Your movement toward the dog, and the reaching action to make the correction, causes some dogs to automatically move away from your reach.

This is where the injuries to the handler's fingers tend to happen. The tab ensures you that this will not happen, as you are actually grabbing a piece of leash rather than the ring of the collar. The tab also serves as a reminder to the dog that the handler is in control.

Down Stay with Food Refusal and Distractions

The food refusal exercise helps to teach the dog not to take food from strangers without the owners permission.

As previously stated, in order to teach a new concept, we will first go back to the basics with the six foot and 30 foot leashes.

Put the dog on a Down Stay and squat down along side him. Have a friend approach and talk to the dog. Correct the dog's intention if you see the slightest indication that he is going to move out of position. Praise him if he stays in place with "Good, Boy. Good Stay."

When you are in the beginning stages of this exercise, work on the typical distractions that the dog might encounter, such as a person approaching and speaking to the dog, clapping hands, throwing toys, or any distraction that seems likely to come up in the future. When you feel that he is distraction-proof, you can begin to proof him on food.

Have a friend approach him with tidbits of food, such as hot dog pieces, while you are squatted down by his side. Have the friend offer him food from the hand first. If the dog looks like he is going to take it, admonish with him with the correction "No" and a jerk on the training collar if necessary. Do this over again until the dog turns his head and refuses the food. Next, have your friend toss the tidbits toward the dog but not directly within his reach. Again, correct the dog if he tries to reach out toward the treats. As the dog begins to understand the rules, the treats should be tossed closer and closer to him until they can be bounced off of his paws without any attempt on his part to retrieve and devour them. When this goal is reached, you can then begin to move further and further away from him while the friend walks out and tosses the treats. The exercise is complete when you can leave the area and stand completely out of site while your friend offers him food and tosses food towards him, while he still refuses to eat it.

Stay and Down on Recall

In the beginning stages of teaching the down on recall it helps the dog to understand what is expected if the handlers body language is exaggerated in stepping forward and pointing down.

By now, your dog should be coming swiftly when you call. But what do you do if you call the dog and you suddenly realize that there is a dangerous situation such as an oncoming car that might hit him? The Stay or Down on the Recall could be a life-saving command.

Begin by using the six foot leash. As you call the dog, step backwards so that he cannot reach you. At any point before he gets to you, command "Stay" and step toward him with your palm out toward him like a traffic cop. As he stops, tell him "Good Stay" and slowly back up to the end of the leash. Praise him for staying, call him to come to you, then finish as though you were working on a regular recall. As he shows an understanding of this routine, you can move to the thirty foot line and then to a light line and tab. Be careful to add a regular recall in at times, or you will get the dog slowing in anticipation every time you call him.

Similarly, the Down on the Recall should be taught first on the six foot leash. Calling the dog and moving backwards, you will then take a step forward, pointing at the dog's paws and commanding "Down." Take a step forward and correct him if necessary.

Then praise "Good Down" as you back up slowly. Call him again and do a regular finish to the heel position. Give him lots of praise for learning and completing this exercise so that he does not become intimidated by not knowing if the routine is going to be a straight recall, down, or stay. You want to make it a game for him and not a point of frustration.

If the dog recalls too quickly for you to give the second command, you can have a helper use a second long line attached to the dog from behind. As the dog comes to you, the second person can slow him down so that he can learn the new exercise.

Sit and Down from a Distance

When teaching the sit from a distance it helps if the handlers body language tells the dog that the desire is to come up and forward which is accomplished by the handler stepping backwards and pointing upwards.

The Sit and Down from a distance is very similar to teach to the Down on Recall.

Beginning with the dog on the end of the six foot leash, give him the Stay command and step to the end of the six foot leash facing him.

Next, step forward with your right foot and right arm extended, while pointing down at his feet command "Down," and then correct in a downward motion if necessary.

Remember to say "No" if you need to correct. Lavish praise on him verbally if he complies. Next, step backward with the same foot, bringing your right hand backward and up, commanding "Sit" and pulling him slightly forward. His own forward motion should bring him to a stand as you point over his head to his rear. Again, correct in an upward motion, saying "No" if he doesn't comply. If he does comply, you will again lavish praise on him verbally. Continue to practice at this distance until you are sure that the dog understands what you desire from him. At this point, you can begin to move further from the dog using the long line, then progress to the light line and tab. You will want to avoid the situation where you have to approach the dog to make the correction, as he will naturally anticipate the correction and may jump back away from you. In order to avoid this circumstance, you should take each step slowly and try not to be impatient.

Stand for Examination

Teaching the stand for the first time is easier for the dog if food is used in front of the dogs nose. This keeps her mind occupied while she is praised for standing in the proper position. Once successful she is more likely to be willing to do it again properly.

The Stand for Examination is necessary when the dog is in competition, but also has its applications for practical purposes such as grooming or examinations by veterinarians. One of the easiest ways to teach this is to slip a leash under the dog's hindquarters.

Once the dog is used to standing and being praised for taking this position, the stay command can be added and the handler can move in a circle around the dog.

Make sure the leash is not overly tight or the dog may panic.

From the Heel position tell the dog to Heel and take two steps forward. After two steps, make a half turn to your left and command the dog to "Stand." As you do so, tighten both of the leashes so that one is holding his head up and the other is holding his hindquarters up. If the dog struggles against the leash on his hindquarters, relax it and attempt to hold him with your left hand where the leash would be. As soon as the dog holds still in the stand position, begin to verbally praise him so that he knows what you are asking him to do. Once you can get across to him that this is what you want, things will get easier each time. This exercise needs to be broken down into segments in order for the dog to learn without stress. The first objective is to teach him what stand means and to simply go from the sitting position to the standing position.

Next, you will want him to be able to stand for a longer period of time while you move around him in a circle. This is a bit of trial and error on his part, as he may try to step forward while you move around him. You will need to tell him to "Stay" as you would with the Sit or Down Stay command, but in this case you may want to keep one hand on his back while you move in a circle. With most dogs, this will help them understand that you are not expecting them to follow you at the Heel position. After you can get around him in a full circle with your hand on his back, you can remove the hand and attempt to do the same thing at the end of the six foot leash.

The most difficult step in this process is the addition of another person, who will come up to the dog and examine him. In obedience competitions held under American Kennel Club standards, this is done by the judge approaching and putting his or her hand on the dog's head, withers, and rear, then stepping away and asking the handler to return to the dog. The dog must not move his feet from the position he is left in at any time until the handler releases him. This exercise is performed off of the leash, but with the handler four to six feet from the dog. For these purposes, it is not necessary for you to practice at a great distance. That being said, some people like to practice the stand stay at a distance, or even teach the change of position by adding stand to the sit and down from a distance exercise. If the Stand command is going to be used to show the dog in conformation shows, food (bait) will be allowed in the ring (AKC), and the dog can be taught that standing still when the handler places (stacks) him or when he is brought in front of the judge, results in the food reward.

Dealing with Distractions

Through the training up to this point, you have corrected your dog for responding to distractions. At this point in your training, you will want to set up scenarios where the dog will learn on his own that *you are the most important person in his life and he should not leave you to seek play or explore other situations.* The way you have been doing this up until now has been to correct him for his desire to explore new situations. At this point in his training, you will do this by *allowing him to explore in controlled situations.*

An example of how you will do this is setting up circumstances with a knowledgeable handler and dog. When you enter the training area, have a toy ready to play with the dog. Have the other handler at the opposite end of the field tossing a toy in the air. As your dog leaves you to approach him to play, he should put the toy away and walk the other direction, ignoring the dog. At this same time, you should call his name and offer him the chance of playing with you. Do this a few times and he will soon learn on his own that you are more important than distractions. The same goes for the distraction of other dogs. For this you will need a seasoned dog that is not aggressive towards other dogs. You will handle this in the exact same way as you did the stranger with the toy; only in this instance it will be a stranger, a dog, and a toy. When your dog tries to approach the other team, they both should pick up their toy and walk away from him. At the same time, you should be calling him and asking him to play. This will resolve any conflict in the dog's mind as to whether it is more fun to stay with you or play with the other dog, handler, and toy. You will never have to deal with this conflict again. You will, of course, not do this if your dog is extremely dog aggressive (aggressive to other dogs) and poses a threat to the other dog and handler. Your dog must be well-trained and socialized to learn in this way.

Agility Training Off-Leash

Agility commands should always be started with a spotter to help to keep the dog from jumping off of ramps and high places. Once the dog is conditioned how to use the agilities the handler can direct the dog from a distance without the help of the spotter.

Now that your dog has off-leash obedience training and has been introduced to some basic agilities on the six and thirty foot leashes, he should be ready to perform these agilities off leash (on the tab) and using voice control only. You can also seek out more agilities for him to practice on. Introducing him to tunnels, weave poles, teeter totters and other agility equipment (used for agility competitions) should be easy for him now. You will want to start him as carefully as you did with your on-leash training, so that he does not become afraid of a piece of equipment or inclined to jump or fall off of it. Because you have established his confidence and your voice control, you should not have any real difficulties with these new experiences.

Protection Training

If you are seriously considering protection training your dog, this point in the dog's life is the age of reckoning. It is at this age that the dog's hormones will kick in and tell him to be more protective of his territory and owner. This is an age where the dog tends to be on a hormonal rollercoaster, one day seeming to act sure of himself and the next seeming overly cautious. This is normal for this age group and can frustrate the owner when it manifests itself in extremes. This is a good time to take the natural aggression that the dog is starting to show and mold it to fit your needs.

If you have been playing tug games with the dog as he has grown up, now is the time to start to work with a professional trainer so that you may teach the dog to use his defense drive in the proper fashion. You should not attempt to do this yourself for several reasons. The most important reason is that if you do this wrong, the dog can become dangerous. The dog needs to learn to "turn on" and "turn off" on command. You should not just practice the easy aggressive part as this can turn into an ugly situation. It is just as important, if not more so, to teach the dog how to control itself by turning off on command. This not only makes the dog safer to have around, but it also provides the precursor to his letting go of the bite. (See Suggested Reading.)

Tracking & Searching

At this point in your dog's development, you will be ready to add more advanced elements of tracking and/or searching, dependent on what your plans are for your dog. In both of these areas, the foundational training should have been established when your dog was under one year old. Now you will want to advance into teaching him to work further away from you and managing things like turns and problem solving. This is the level of training where you begin to set up for an actual title or certification.

Since this book is limited in its scope, we would direct you toward both the Suggested Reading Section and Chapter XII: Beyond the Basics (Titles and Certifications), where you will find various resources that you can utilize to train further towards your goals in these areas.

X. DEALING WITH DOMINANCE AND AGGRESSION ISSUES

There are a variety of reasons why dogs become aggressive. Some reasons have genetic foundations, others medical, and still others have their roots in behaviors that are learned from other dogs or people.

It is for these reasons that we generally look towards eliminating the medical aspects first when training a dog that is overly aggressive. Why do we eliminate the medical causes first? Because, if the root of the problem is medical, no amount of training will ever

Dogs left to grow up without an education can often act like street thugs.

completely solve the problem. There is no doubt that rehabilitation will necessitate training as part of the solution, because of the many learned behaviors associated with the aggression. If the dog's problem has its foundation in pain, it is unfair to the dog to put it through training which could exacerbate the problem and cause the dog more discomfort. It is for this reason that all underlying health issues, such as Hip Dysplasia, a broken or impacted tooth, or a hormone imbalance, need to be identified and dealt with first prior to training. Training the dog prior to dealing with the health issue will put the dog in more pain and can potentially put the trainer in danger. The dog only has one way to defend himself against something that hurts and this is to growl or threaten. The misunderstanding of this natural reaction has seen many dogs with physical maladies put down or given away.

When an owner comes to see us with an adult dog that has been displaying aggression or has bitten someone, the first thing we generally do is suggest a visit to the veterinarian. We suggest a full set of x-rays, including hips, elbows, and spine. This is done to make sure that there is no hip or elbow dysplasia, or arthritis in the spine or tail bone that is causing aggression.

While the dog is under anesthesia for the x-rays, we suggest that the veterinarian do a full examination of the teeth to make sure the dog does not have a toothache. In addition, the veterinarian should draw blood and send it to the lab to be checked for thyroid disorders or other chemical imbalances, such as excessive testosterone. If the dog is male and the problems are not obvious in the x-rays and dental examination, it is advisable to have the dog neutered unless the veterinarian finds something that requires consultation prior to surgery. It takes three months for the testosterone to fully leave a male dog's system after neutering, so a second evaluation by the trainer may be required at that time.

The importance of veterinary evaluation is well-represented by a dog that was brought to us named "Samson." Samson was a two year old male Rottweiler owned by a brother and sister that were both in law enforcement. Their father, who had also been a police officer, had been given the dog as a puppy while he was bed-ridden due to cancer. Since their father had passed away, the dog had been moody and often tried to bite guests when they came to the house. He would also growl at the family members when they asked him to go outside or get off of the couch. The owners stated that getting rid of him in any fashion was not an option, as this was the last link they had with their father, who had truly loved the dog.

Upon evaluation, "Samson" seemed friendly but was notably guarded when asked to interact with the trainer. He held his head down and rolled his eyes upwards to watch the trainer in a classic self-protective posture. As part of the consultation with the owners, we suggested that they have the aforementioned tests done on the dog to rule out pain or a chemical imbalance.

They surprised us by saying that they had already done this when "Samson" was six months old. When we inquired as to why the veterinarian would have done x-rays on such a young puppy, they stated that the veterinarian had suspected that something was wrong with his hips. When we asked what the outcome of those tests was, they stated that they were unsure. We then asked for permission to call the veterinarian to inquire. When we got the veterinarian on the phone, he stated "What part of bilateral hip dysplasia did they not understand?" Of course, at this point, training the dog was out of the question, as it was clear that his problems were not behavioral, but medical. The owners told us that they had "blocked" the bad news when they heard it eighteen months prior because their father was dying, and they didn't want to add a crisis with his dog to the mix. We sent them to a specialist, who reported that the dog also had bilateral elbow dysplasia, so there was literally no place for the dog to put his weight without extreme pain. Had we agreed to train this dog, it would have been pure torture for him, and he probably would have bitten one of his trainers. This is why the medical health of the dog is so important to consider when training. Eventually, the owners happily paid for replacement surgery on each of the dog's joints. The bill amounted to $15,000.00, but they spent many years with the dog that had made their father happy in the last days of his life. There is no price tag too high for love and personal attachments.

Aggression in a case such as Samson's is biologically hard-wired into the dog. In the wild, a dog in this kind of pain would not last long. This is nature's way of culling the animals that should not procreate. Samson would not have been long for this world had he needed to hunt for his meals and travel for miles, as wolves and wild dogs do. Dogs know that they need to cover up their maladies and attempt not to show them so that they will not be attacked by predators or even their own pack in a mercy killing.

It is for this reason that humans often do not recognize the maladies in their dogs, since the owner expects the dog to cry or whine if he is hurting. The dog is naturally stoic when in pain, because showing it would be a sign of weakness that would be recognizable by other animals and dangerous to his survival.

Because of this self-protective nature in the dog he often makes a good offense his best defense. This is why Samson would growl at his owners when they asked him to get up or go out. Rather than whine to say "it hurts," he growled to say "leave me alone."

A dog in pain will not want to get up and move around once he is lying down. It takes some momentum to get him going. Anyone who has experienced surgery or arthritis should be able to identify with this feeling. The other sign of pain is the *drooped head.*

If the dog's head is held below the shoulders when he stands or walks, this is a sign that he doesn't feel good. A healthy dog should walk with his head up and show an alert and eager attitude.

It is very unfortunate that dogs are often corrected severely for aggression that is pain-based. In some cases, people even take the dog and drop it off at the pound when it growls or snaps at a family member. The dog may just have a simple ear infection or a bad tooth. We have seen this happen many times, even with normally diligent dog owners who simply misread what their dog is trying to convey to them. It is important to realize that the dog has few ways of conveying pain or discomfort to you. Beyond the obvious limp, he can only become stoic, growl, or snap. *Whining or crying in dogs is usually only the result of nerve pain* (such as when you step on a dog's toe) and should not be expected if the dog is dealing with a chronic ache. Most often, the dog will simply learn to live with it. This, however, can, and usually does, result in aggressive behavior for the sake of compensating for the pain.

Other problems that may result in pain-based aggression include growing pains which can occur in young dogs (usually around 6-12 months of age) and severe matting of the fur. Matting of the fur can become so severe that it will rip the skin and cause infection. Many people with long-coated breeds do not understand the upkeep that is necessary for the dog's health. Regular brushing and visits to the groomer are a necessary part of owning some breeds. If the owner does not wish to maintain this type of grooming schedule with the dog, it is best to shave them down to a manageable length so that the dog can be bathed at home and the hair cannot mat.

Unfortunately, neglect and ignorance when it comes to a dog's health and welfare are fairly common occurrences among many dog owners. We are consistently amazed at how many people will treat a trainer or kennel owner as a one stop shop. Though most owners intuitively know that there are some basic elements of upkeep that need to be tended to for their pet's sake, they often ignore them in the hopes that a trained professional can do all of the work for them. Some owners have to be told that the dog needs to see a veterinarian for an open wound or visit a groomer because of severe mats.

Neurological Causes Of Aggression

Without a doubt, the most dangerous disorder a trainer or owner can face in a dog is "Rage Syndrome." This is a neurological disorder in the emotional lobe of the brain. As an analog, think of motor epilepsy, where misfiring in the brain causes physical seizures that you can readily observe. Rage Syndrome is caused by the same type of misfiring, with the exception that it occurs in the emotional lobe of the dog and causes aggressive outbursts. This is sometime referred to as "Jekyll and Hyde" behavior or "Springer Rage" (because it is a condition that seems to often occur in Springer Spaniels). Thankfully, this condition is not common, though it is very dangerous when it occurs. In large breeds it can even be lethal to the human victim.

It takes a veterinarian who specializes in Neurology to diagnose Rage Syndrome, and owners will often not realize the condition's existence without this help. What eventually points the veterinarian or trainer towards a diagnosis of Rage Syndrome is a reoccurrence of unexplainable aggression. When this develops into a pattern, a veterinarian or trainer might start to suspect Rage Syndrome. To complicate the situation, the owner often makes the mistake of rationalizing away the dog's behavior. When such clients visit our facility for a consultation, they will generally say something like "Uncle Bob had been petting him for a good ten minutes before he tried to attack him, but uncle Bob had been drinking and was talking loudly so he probably didn't trust him." It is only when a skilled listener begins to pull information out of the client that you can start to put the pieces of the puzzle together and realize that this has been an ongoing problem. Another reason that owners will often not be completely honest with the trainer about the dog's history is because they do not want to prejudice the trainer against the dog in advance of the training. The obvious problem with this idea is that the owner is thereby putting the trainer in danger by not revealing all of the information necessary for the trainer to make a proper evaluation of how dangerous the dog may be. In addition, the dog with rage syndrome is often very approachable and even loving. Because of the nature of Rage Syndrome the dog acts normal 98% of the time. The dog may be very affectionate and appear to be safe with strangers and even small children. When the seizure in the brain takes place, there are no outward signs like there would be with motor epilepsy. The dog simply changes from sweet and loving into a vicious attack dog without warning.

As terrible as this may sound, let us reassure you that Rage Syndrome is rare. In twenty-seven years and after training approximately 20,000 dogs, we have seen only about a dozen cases. The variety of dogs we have seen it in has included Springer Spaniels, Golden Retrievers, German Shepherds, Dobermans, and a Newfoundland.

This neurological disorder is possible in any breed, but highly improbable. Rage Syndrome should not be confused with epilepsy in the behavioral lobe. It is in fact epilepsy in the emotional lobe. There is such a thing as epilepsy in the behavioral lobe, which does not cause the dog to be aggressive, but rather causes him to act strangely, as though he is hallucinating. Evidence of this condition would be shadow chasing, chasing of imaginary flies, fixation on novel objects, scratching at imaginary objects, and standing on hind legs and spinning while looking into the sky.

Dogs with epilepsy in the behavioral lobe can be intelligent and train well, but will be seen from time to time displaying these odd behaviors. One of the worst cases we have seen of a dog with epilepsy in the behavioral lobe (as diagnosed later by a neurologist) was a Golden Retriever named "Simba." Simba's owners lived in Huntington Beach, right on the water. They had hired a trainer to train with them in their home when Simba was six months old. The trainer had become so frustrated trying to train Simba that he had given up after a few weeks. Simba's owners reported that this poor man was baffled and quite embarrassed that he could not get this six month old Golden Retriever to complete a Down/Stay command. In addition, the trainer could not understand or give any explanation for some of the behaviors that Simba was displaying. Several times when he tried to get the dog to Down/Stay, the dog would act as though he was just stung by a bee. He would suddenly jump up and tuck his tail as if he was stung. He would whirl around and look at his rear end as if the offending bee could be seen. He would also watch the imaginary bee on the rare occasion that he maintained the down stay. His head would follow an imaginary flight pattern that would make even the most cynical person believe that there was indeed a bee present.

As Simba grew older, he began to display behaviors that were even more perplexing. He would be outside in the backyard, relaxed and sleeping, when suddenly he would jump up for no apparent reason and attack his owner's French doors, scratching furiously at them while standing on his hind legs. He would then suddenly stop and go back to lying down and sleeping.

The owners finally resorted to putting Plexiglas over the doors to protect them.

The final straw for the owners occurred when their teenage daughter took Simba for a walk next to the seawall. During their walks the dog would periodically stand up on his back legs and begin scratching at them as though he was trying to get something off of them. It didn't happen every time they walked, and they didn't see it as a danger until Simba did this to their daughter and managed to push her over the seawall in the process. She found herself and the dog in the water. She was startled to say the least and afraid that the dog was going to swim at her and drown her. Luckily he had snapped out of his episode when they hit the water and did not continue to try to scratch her.

We agreed to take in the dog for observation and training. Simba was placed in a run that had a door leading from the inside to the outside. It wasn't long before we heard a loud banging noise coming from the kennel. We rushed out to observe Simba, finding him pushing the door open and closed over and over again with his paws. We then changed him to an inside only run. It wasn't long before we heard a loud scratching noise. Again, we rushed out to observe

Simba leaning against the side wall of the kennel while standing on his pallet, scratching at it as though he was trying to dig to China. When we spoke to him, he seemed not to hear us as he was so focused on his scratching. After about a minute, he suddenly noticed us and approached the door with his tail wagging. Within thirty seconds, his head snapped back toward the pallet, and he ran back and resumed his scratching.

We consulted a veterinarian who had pioneered the use of Prozac on both coasts, and he suggested the use of Prozac, as he felt that this was an obsessive compulsive disorder. We put Simba on Prozac while we were obedience training him and were able to complete all of the commands, but Simba still appeared to hallucinate, although he was just happily hallucinating. Simba still had the same odd behaviors as he had prior to being prescribed the Prozac. He could be obedience-trained, but you would have to allow for the odd behaviors in the midst of his routine.

We didn't feel that the Prozac was really the answer for him, so we sought out the help of a neurologist. The neurologist put Simba through a few tests that proved to him that the signals from Simba's brain were not reaching his rear end properly. He explained to us and Simba's owner that his brain was misfiring in the *Behavioral Lobe* and causing his odd behavior. Unlike the misfiring in the *Emotional Lobe*, which is dangerous, the *Behavioral Lobe* misfiring only causes odd behaviors. Simba was put on Phenobarbital, and his dosage was monitored according to effect. We finished his training with an 80% improvement in his odd behaviors, which was enough for the owners to feel like they could live with him for the rest of his life.

Conclusion

As you can see, there can be many medical causes that can affect behaviors and aggression in dogs. The well-informed owner and trainer will eliminate these factors or deal with them from a medical perspective prior to or at least during training. It is not fair to the dog, owner, or trainer, to proceed in treating aggression problems through training alone if the root cause of the problem might be medical. The use of medication can help to alleviate pain or anxiety in the dog. This will help the owners to get the results that they desire and help to lessen the chances of the trainer being hurt in the process due to the dog biting defensively.

Fear Aggression (Anxiety Driven Aggression)

Fear aggression is one of the most common forms of aggression that we see as trainers. There are two basic types of fear aggression

1) Learned: due to abuse, neglect, trauma, or lack of socialization
2) Genetic: Stemming from a weak nervous system that puts the dog in a constant state of anxiety.

In many cases there is a combination of factors at work. For the trainer, the challenge is to know how to best unravel which factors are the root causes and know how best to treat the dog in order to produce the best results.

In general, the best course of action for a fear-aggressive dog is a combination of calming the nerves with the temporary use of anti-anxiety medication (human grade such as Elavil works best in our experience) prescribed by a veterinarian (appropriate to dogs that are harmful to themselves or others) and *to socialize the dog properly outside of the presence of its owners.* This helps teach the dog to have confidence in itself and stand on its own four feet, separate from the owner. This is best done in a kennel environment where multiple people handle the dog and it is necessary to work around multiple dogs. For the very fearful dog, this process may need to be broken into segments.

It is important for owners of fear-aggressive dogs to understand that while significant improvement may be possible with training and therapy, the best advice for them is to manage the dog in a way that lessens the stress in its life. This means avoiding situations that the dog finds stressful to the greatest extent possible. For instance, if the dog is fearful of loud noises, it would be prudent to bring the dog inside in a crate on the Fourth of July. This way the dog will not hurt itself trying to break out of the yard or into the house. If you play music or turn on the television to provide cover noise, the dog may not even hear the fireworks outside. You may even consider tranquilizers prescribed by a veterinarian for temporary use in such a situation.

Forcing the dog into social settings is usually not recommended for fear-aggressive dogs. By forcing the dog to deal with situations such as parties at your home, you heighten the anxiety level unnecessarily and increase the possibility of a guest being bitten. In many cases, you can solve a potential problem by simply avoiding the situation.

Some dogs have natural social boundaries. While they can learn to accept a handful of social settings, such as walking in the park, it is entirely another thing to be approached and petted by strangers. Just as some people are uncomfortable being hugged or touched by people outside of their inner circle, some dogs will not accept being touched by strangers.

Ask yourself what can be gained versus what can be lost in any situation. Because you are liable for your dog's behavior, in most cases you have more to lose. It is much easier to ask strangers not to pet him because he is fearful of strangers. This is better than saying he might bite. The best protection against a mishap is to simply not put the dog in this situation in the first place.

Defensive Aggression (High Defense Drive) Anti-Social Behavior

Many people are confused by the defensive drive in dogs. People tend to want to classify defensive dogs as "mean." This label is in reality a misinterpretation of the drive called *defense*. Dogs, by their nature, have various levels of defense and prey drives. If they had to survive in the wild, the defense drive would be utilized to defend food, pups, territory, and place in the pack.

Prey drive would be used for hunting. It is the drive to hunt, chase, struggle, and apprehend prey. These drives have been bred into or out of various breeds of dogs throughout human history. Humans have tinkered with dogs' drives in order to make them more useful for their own purposes. In the case of working breeds, such as German Shepherds or Belgian Malinois (to name two of the most popular police dogs), both drives are bred high in these breeds so that they will make good patrol candidates. This does not, however, indicate that these dogs are *mean*.

The conventional notion that dogs are not born "mean," but that people make them "mean" is often true. This does not apply at all, however, to defense drives. Dogs *are* born either with high, medium, or low drives. This is a genetic predisposition. A good example of this is two dogs that we owned, "Nana" and "Kimba." Nana was Kimba's aunt, as Kimba was a puppy of Nana's sister. Nana was Schutzhund (obedience, tracking, & protection) trained and titled, as was Kimba's mother. Nana and her sister were both very social animals who put on demonstrations and competed in front of crowds. Although you could watch either of these females do full protection work to a very high level, they were extremely accessible to strangers.

They were both dogs with a high level of tolerance for socialization. Nana and her sister were both very high in their prey drives, which empowered them to do all of the work required by Schutzhund but still allowed them to be social. Nana would bark when someone was approaching and would consistently protect her yard. During a work day, she would let a dozen people walk in and out of her yard while she played with her toy. She unnerved a few people who dared to walk through her yard carrying a towel or wearing gardening gloves, as she saw these as prey items and would attack the items (an important distinction, since she was not actually attacking *the people*). She simply wanted to possess the gloves, but try telling that to someone when they have an eighty pound dog hanging from their hand. She wouldn't bite down hard, and at the end of her life she barely had any teeth from chewing on her toys. We would have to yell "give her the glove," and as soon as they slid the glove from their hand she would happily run off with the glove in her mouth. This demonstrates how high her prey drive was. Remember that prey drive is the drive to chase, apprehend, and possess things.

The behavior of Kimba couldn't have been in sharper contrast to Nana's. One half of her genetic makeup was identical to Nana. Nana's father was also a Schutzhund dog. Kimba was raised, trained, and socialized by our friend and associate, Ivan Balabanov, until she was close to one year old. He was raising Kimba with the intent of channeling her drives into Schutzhund. He found her to be too high in her defense drives and called us to see if we would be interested in her, as he knew that we did police and security work with our dogs.

It soon became obvious that her temperament was such that she was too high in defense to be a good Schutzhund candidate. By contrast, we owned her litter brother, who was balanced in his drives and a better candidate for Schutzhund so we did a swap.

In her life with us, Kimba slept under our bed at night. She played with our children and would roll over on her back and let them lie on her and hug her. She was, however, completely unapproachable by our staff or any stranger while in her yard, run or crate, unless she was on the leash and under our control. She was totally safe in obedience and protection exercises and would simply ignore onlookers, but that was only as the result of much practice. There was a strict rule at our facility that no one was to enter her kennel but our family. At one point, one of our long-time trainers decided that she was the exception to this rule. She felt that the dog knew her well enough to allow the trainer to move her out of the kennel. The result of that fateful decision was twenty-five stitches in her arm. This was the second time in twenty-seven years that we had to drive an employee to the emergency room.

Kimba later had a litter of pups, a group which possessed a wide variety of temperaments. One of her puppies became a Champion, attained her obedience and agility titles, and became a Schutzhund 3 (German Dog Sport involving obedience, tracking, and protection). Her temperament was not like Kimba, but rather closer to her grandmother's and great aunt's. The lesson that you should take from this example is that even dogs from the same litter or line can have totally different temperaments. They may throw back to an ancestor that has a different temperament than the parents. The important thing is for the owner to recognize the strengths and weaknesses of their dog and to deal with them accordingly. If the dog is not suitable for your purposes, there probably is someone out there that the dog is perfect for. You shouldn't make the mistake of trying to change the dog's personality, as this is no more possible than someone changing your personality. It is true that dogs can learn new behaviors, but what nature has provided at the core of a dog's being will always be there.

In Kimba's example, she would submit herself to our will when she was under our command. Left to her own devices, she would revert back to her old defensive nature. Dogs are, at their core, the product of their genetic makeup.

High Prey Drive: The Drive To Chase, Apprehend, Struggle & Posses

Another commonly misunderstood drive in dogs is prey drive. This is the natural drive to chase, apprehend, struggle with, and posses prey. We have all seen dogs that will endlessly chase a ball to the point of exhaustion (high prey drive) or bite and fight with a tug endlessly. On the opposite end of the scale are dogs that couldn't care less about chasing a ball. They look at you as though saying "you go fetch the ball." What you are observing in these situations is the level of the dog's prey drive.

Prey drive is utilized by humans in many ways such as:
Herding: The dog runs after the sheep and nips at their heels.

Gun Dogs: The dog runs after and retrieves birds.
Terriers: The dog chases and kills vermin.
Hounds: The dog chases and traps quarry.
Police Dogs: The dog chases and apprehends the bad guy.

All of these are examples of natural prey drive which is channeled into tasks that benefit human beings. These drives are not *created* by humans, but rather harnessed by them. It is true that humans can create dogs that have higher prey drive than others through selective breeding, but humans do not create the prey drive themselves. It is either present or it is not.

The novice dog owner often misunderstands prey drive as something dangerous. When the puppy shows a tendency to run after the children and bite at their ankles, the owner may make the mistake of thinking that the dog will grow up to be a danger.

Playful biting is a natural way for the puppy to explore its world and express the natural prey drives that it possesses. The puppy simply needs to be redirected to an appropriate toy.

Another urban legend is that once a dog tastes blood it will become vicious. We can tell you that we have received a number of calls over the years from frantic owners after a dog has killed a cat or a chicken and the owner is just sure that since "he has tasted blood" that he is now going to "turn on" family members. The chase and kill instinct towards prey animals is a natural occurrence in canines. It is a natural reflex in the dog, which simply demonstrates the level of his prey drive: nothing more, nothing less. If the dog has been safe in the past with family members, he will continue to be so. If he was already showing problems in this area, then one can reasonably suspect that the killing of an animal may show that his prey drives are too high to allow him around young children that may run and scream and, in general, act like prey. However, there are usually multiple factors involved in cases such as these beyond the prey drive.

Prey drive has no malice behind it. It is a survival drive that is hard-wired into the dog. The dog chases for the pure pleasure of the hunt and, occasionally, to eat. He hunts for the same reasons that humans hunt: for food and/or sport.

Dominance-Related Aggression

One of the most prevalent problems we see with owners and dogs is dominance-related aggression.

The majority of these problems are actually caused by the owners.

This is due to the fact that many owners do not understand the dog's hardwired need to know who is in charge and where his place in the pack is at all times. The dog's pack does not just relate to the other dogs he lives with, but also to the humans in the household as well. The pack order is easiest to establish right away with the new puppy or dog. If the dog becomes the pack leader in the household, there will be a struggle to change the order of things later. This is why it is so crucial to train puppies at a young age and not to wait until things get out of hand. Changing the pack order with an older dog can at times become dangerous.

One common mistake that people make is spoiling the dog. People usually do this with the misguided assumption that giving the dog everything he wants and more will establish a greater bond of love between them. In reality, giving the dog everything that it wants whenever it wants things (such as treats, praise, attention, or sleeping on the bed), all lead to convincing the dog that he is in charge. Sleeping in bed with the owner can give the dog an unhealthy attachment to the owner and oftentimes results in aggression to a spouse, due to a heightened sense of the dog's pack position. Sooner or later, the spoiling will escalate to the dog giving orders to the owner in his own language. This presents itself as growling because he doesn't want to get off the bed or go outside, barking to come in or out, guarding food or toys, rushing in or out of doors in front of the owner, etc. To the dog this is normal behavior, because in his world the Alpha gets everything it wants first and only gives up possessions when it wants to. The Alpha is the first dog to engage in a fight when an intruder comes into its territory. This is why a fight sometimes breaks out between dogs when guarding at a fence. This is also why a fight may break out between dogs when the owner steps out the door to give their dogs attention, a new toy, or a treat. It is at these times that the Alpha must make sure that the other dogs respect him. When a visitor comes in the house, the Alpha may run to the door to challenge them or snap at them in some form while they are in the house. This is his way of establishing with the visitor that this is his house and that the visitor is not welcome as he is not a member of the pack.

For a trainer it is a frustration to be brought a two to three year old dog that has been building his Alpha position for years. Usually something has happened in the household that has become a catalyst to seek help. The reason is often a nip or a bite on a visitor or child. Because the dog was not trained when it was young, the training will be much harder on everyone concerned. The dog will have to have his whole way of thinking changed. He must learn to submit himself to his owner's wishes. The owner must learn a totally new way of thinking and behaving towards the dog. The trainer may find himself or herself in harm's way while managing the situation. If the trainer does decide to take on this problem, the first order of business is to make sure that the dog is neutered if it is a male. Testosterone acts like a turbo-booster for aggression and should be done away with for everyone's sake. It takes three months after neutering a male dog for the testosterone to diminish. If the dog is dangerous, we suggest neutering the animal and then waiting three months before reevaluating him for training. If he is trainable and only moderately aggressive, the training can be started as soon as the dog recovers from the surgery.

If the situation is deemed this dangerous, our recommendation to the owner is to do one of three things: Put the dog down, keep the dog in a locked dog run except when it is out with adults who can handle the dog on a leash and while wearing a muzzle in public, or relocate the dog to a business situation where it lives behind a fence and is charged with protecting personal property.

Many dominant dogs are approachable when they are not under the stress of being asked to do something. The first test of whether a dog is acceptable in training will be whether or not he will be approachable in the kennel. He must be able to be moved from place to place in the kennel environment without danger to the staff.

Double Leash (Training with Caveat)
After it is determined that the dog can be approachable and moved from place to place, the next question will be how the dog behaves when he is corrected. This is where it is important for the trainer to protect himself by using a double leash or a muzzle.

Since the first reaction to the muzzle is generally for the dog to fight it and try to get it off, it is less stressful on the dog to begin with a double leash. The double leash consists of two leashes attached to two slip collars (choke chains) around the dog's neck at the same time. One is held by a trainer on the left of the dog and the other by the primary trainer, who stands to the dog's right. The trainer on the left of the dog is there simply to protect the other trainer if the dog should try to attack him. The trainer on the left has a thirty foot leash so that he can be further away (approximately six to ten feet) from the dog and therefore remain less obtrusive throughout the process. The trainer on the right of the dog will carry out the lesson as usual. The trainer on the left must always stay parallel to the trainer on the right with the leash tight enough to be ready to pull the dog away if he tries to attack the trainer on the right. The leash must not be so tight that it hinders the training or distracts the dog. When the dog is given a correction, the second test as to whether the dog can be trained will take place. If the dog takes the correction from the primary trainer and goes on with the lesson, it is a good sign that he will be trainable without danger.

If he becomes aggressive to the primary trainer but realizes after the correction that intimidating the trainer will not work and goes on with the lesson, he will be trainable (albeit with a great deal of caution).

If he explodes aggressively and tries to attack the trainer and upon correction tries to bite the leash and chokes himself while struggling between the double leashes, he will shut down and not be trainable. This is usually a dog that has high aggression coupled with weak nerves. This is a very dangerous animal because when he becomes aggressive he shuts off his thinking process and simply reacts. This is somewhat like the raging bull that cannot be stopped once he is enraged.

The type of dog that shuts off and goes into a blind rage is the dog you see on the six o'clock news after attacking an innocent person. This is usually a combination of genetics, lack of training and insufficient socialization that combine to make this dog a time bomb. The absolute last chance for this dog is an attempt to train him using sedatives.

The sedation will calm his nerves, which is the catalyst to shutting him down when he fights correction. By calming his nerves there is a chance that the trainer can teach him without the dog throwing the shut-off switch. If this works, the practical recommendation for the dog is to see a veterinarian for long term use of anti-anxiety medication, work toward training him with a muzzle, and to keep the dog in a dog run and away from children and the public. If the dog cannot be trained, even under a mild sedative, he should be euthanized, as he will be uncontrollable when he is in a rage and may even redirect aggression on the owner given the right set of circumstances.

We generally double leash for the first week and slowly introduce the dog to the muzzle by putting it on for short periods and then rewarding the dog with food and praise for leaving it on without a fight. We gradually walk him a few steps with it on and then stop and reward. By the end of the week, if he does not panic with the muzzle on, we begin to do obedience routines, which keep him moving so that he does not have the chance to try to remove the muzzle. At this time the trainer can begin to use the single leash, as he is protected from harm. By the end of the third week, the decision will be made as to whether the muzzle needs to be used long-term.

Honesty is very important when you take an aggressive dog to a trainer. You can be putting people in harm's way if you do not disclose the entire history of what has transpired in the dog's past. A previous case of ours bears this principle out:

A couple came to us with an unaltered male Rottweiler that was show-quality and out of a top working and show line. We had several telephone conversations with the wife prior to two consultations held in person.

During all of these conversations the wife never mentioned that she had been bitten in the face by the dog when he was eleven months old, requiring fourteen stitches in the aftermath. She only mentioned that the dog (who was now two years old) had been in several training programs without success because of his dominant nature. Because the dog was a beautiful example of a Rottweiler in conformation (breed standard), they wanted to attempt to train him without neutering him in case they wanted to show him for a championship. During training he attempted to bite one of the trainers and we used the aforementioned methods very successfully. It wasn't until after we had a trainer nearly bitten by the dog, and until we had been successful in our training, that the women finally told us about the bite to her face. She had knowingly put our staff in danger in order to keep us from being prejudiced against the dog. Of course, we told them that the dog needed to be neutered and insisted that they keep the dog muzzled while in public and even while she trained him in the beginning for her own safety. She had been spoiling him since he was a pup and had given him strong signals that he was the leader of the house. Because he was from a strong working line, he was more than happy to take on the role of leader around the house and that included putting the owner in her place.

In this case, as in others similar to it, teaching the owners to apply ritual behaviors is key to their success. Ritual behaviors are routines that the dog must follow daily, which keep his position in the pack in a subservient position. The typical rituals we teach are stopping at doors and gates, stopping at specific boundaries in the house or at the street until released, and coming in and lying down in a specific "place" in the house designated by the owner. All of these ritual behaviors remind the dog who is in charge on a daily basis.

In the aforementioned case, the owner, once bitten, was afraid of the dog and projected this to him. He saw this as a sign of weakness, which supported his dominance. Once the muzzle was applied, the owner was no longer fearful and could apply correction without fear of being bitten. Part of the problem that had existed between her and the dog was supported by the style of training that she had been applying prior to coming to our facility. The style of training she had been using was food-based and included no correction.

Given that the temperament of the dog was a 9½ on the scale (see temperament scale), she was unknowingly supporting the dog's Alpha position by using this method. He had learned what the five basic commands were and knew how to obtain the food from her, but in his mind *he was manipulating her* in order to obtain the food reward. Since he was never given correction, nor were any boundaries set for his behavior, he assumed the Alpha position. When his owner learned how to change her behavior toward the dog, she learned how to successfully live in harmony with her as the leader.

One of the things that owners have to learn is that taking control of a dog does not mean that the dog will not love them. It actually works in reverse. With proper discipline, the *dog will love you and respect you as the Alpha, and he won't have to live with the conflict of constantly trying to maintain control.* Much like raising children, parents (like owners) often mistake spoiling for showing love. *In reality, both dogs and children need boundaries set for them to feel loved.* We can always tell how hard or easy it is going to be to teach owners this principle based upon how their children behave. After training, many of our clients joke that they need to bring their children in for training. Many people over the years have remarked that training a dog should be a pre-requisite for young couples to have children. The act of being responsible for another life, taking care of health, safety, welfare, and upbringing (training) of another life is an eye-opening experience. Being involved in this process with a dog is a great experience for a teenager.

Dog Aggression

The body language of the dog in the foreground is classic posturing. This dog is showing the dog he is meeting that he is dominant. The erect tail, stiff body posture, and high head hold with ears forward are all dog signals of dominance.

Dog aggression (being aggressive to other dogs) comes in many forms and stems from a variety of circumstances. In some cases, this aggression stems from a traumatic experience such as being attacked by

By contrast the black dog shows submissive posture seen by the lowered tail set, the tucked body posture, and the ears in the backward position.

an older dog when the dog was a puppy. When this is the case, the dog's response is based in fear. He may have decided that the best defense is a good offense. In other cases, the aggression may come out of an inability to understand basic social signals because the puppy was not kept with his litter long enough or was born as a single puppy. In yet other cases, the root cause may be dominance and the need to show other dogs that he controls his environment and that other dogs are not welcome on his turf or around his food, toys, or owners.

Because of the variables, every situation is unique. In some cases, dog aggression can be changed and in other cases it cannot. In general, it is easier to deal with rehabilitation if the root cause is fear rather than dominance. Dominance relates back to the natural pack order of things, and while dogs can be expected to submit in the presence of a human Alpha and be obedient in a pack situation, it is a dangerous experiment to expect them to get along when the human Alpha is not present.

Because dogs are social creatures, they can and oftentimes do enjoy playing together in groups. The most successful groups are dogs with equally social natures and that lack the need to dominate the group. It is true that a skillful trainer who establishes himself or herself as the pack leader can manage a group of dogs together with dominant tendencies by disciplining the pack together as an Alpha wolf would. The question then becomes what happens with the group when this Alpha figure steps out of the picture.

You may remember the old saying that "nature abhors a vacuum." This saying is true with a pack of dogs. Whenever a pack leader is not present, the dogs will re-evaluate the pack and another leader will establish himself. Among dominant dogs there will likely be a fight for this position. The fight can be a bloodless one or a very violent one that results in injury or death. We are often asked the "What if" question by owners. "What if I adopt another dog? Will my dog get along with it." "What if I bring home a puppy? Will my dog accept it or will he be jealous?" This reminds us of a training seminar we attended back in the 1980s where many of the top trainers in the country gathered together to learn some training techniques from top French trainers. During a question and answer period various trainers would ask "What if the dog does this?" "What if he does that?" "What would you do if the dog did this?" After awhile it became a joke in the room as every answer to the question was "It depends on the dog!" At the end of about six "what if" questions, the whole room broke into a chorus saying "It depends on the dog!" Everyone in the room became amused by this as the obvious became glaringly apparent. You cannot answer a hypothetical question about a dog unless you have an insight into the nature of the dog you are asking the question about. This is true of dealing with any dog, or human for that matter. An experienced trainer knows this and has several tools in their training tool box to apply to different situations based on both the dog's temperament and the situation. The novice trainer with only a few tools in his toolbox may attempt to apply the same method to every dog and every situation. This may work with some dogs and backfire with others. All dogs do not respond equally well to the same techniques for a variety of reasons. This is why training is more of an art than a science.

The subject of dog aggression is complex. It depends highly on the individual dog and the circumstances that the dog lives in, as well as the owner's relationship to the dog and understanding of pack structure. Some dogs can be rehabilitated with a slow progression of introduction to other dogs using confinement conditioning and short periods of time being worked and walked together. Other dogs, due to their dominant nature, will never be able to be kept with any other dogs of the same sex.

An example of the variables at work here are the relationships between people. Think of people who are thrown together in a social setting, such a business conference. Much like a dog show or agility trial, these people are busy and focused on events and activities so they don't have much time to worry about their relationships to the others who are involved. If you take the same group of people or dogs and put them in a social setting where they are expected to work as a team and interact with each other or socialize with each other (such as some popular reality television shows), you suddenly have personality conflicts and attempts by some of the parties to gain control over the group. Friendships may form in some cases and conflicts of personality will arise in others. Just as people in a social setting may get in a verbal confrontation or even an all out physical fight, dogs in the same situation may react similarly. The stronger the conflict between two individuals, the harder it will be to convince them that they should get along.

Dogs should always be introduced to each other outside of their territory. The added stress of defending one's territory just adds to the possibility of hostility. In addition, it is a great help to have enclosures for both dogs where they can see each other and get used to each other's presence prior to being loose together. Avoid giving the dogs food, toys, or attention while they are together, as any of these things can be the catalyst to aggression due to jealousy.

It is not uncommon for our clients to request that we introduce their new dogs while at our facility. This generally works well, as they are in neutral territory and away from their owners who they may be jealous over.

Doggy Day Care is another good place to introduce dogs, as it too is neutral territory where the owners are absent.

If you already own a dog that is dominant and you wish to add another dog to your family, you are much more likely to be successful with a dog of the opposite sex. This is because the dog is much more likely to see the new dog as a potential mate rather than a rival. If you already have two or more dogs at home, then you are best off choosing the opposite sex of the most dominant pre-existing dog in the pack.

Many people who have multiple dogs of dominant breeds will house them separately in kennel runs and only let the dogs that get along well run together. There are two positive aspects to this manner of handling things:

1. If the dogs are dominant working dogs, this allows them all to be trained on equal footing for patrol or protection. If they ran in a pack together one dominant dog would emerge and squelch the others' abilities to perform.

2. Every time you allow the dogs to run in the yard after confinement, you are essentially giving them a renewed experience in the yard. They are less likely to be bored and therefore less likely to be destructive or attempt to escape the yard.

Our rule of thumb is to let adults out for long stretches, as they are conditioned and non-destructive, while the younger dogs run for shorter periods since they will become bored sooner and are more prone to destruction.

There are always those individuals who will not own dogs unless they can get along in a pack. These folks must be ready to separate or re-home dogs that will not fit in. The following are ways of introducing new dogs to your pack with as little chance of confrontation as possible:

1. Bring in less dominant and opposite sex dogs to lessen the chances of conflict.
2. Introduce the dogs in neutral territory.
3. Rather than standing still and letting the two dogs go nose to nose upon meeting, consider going for a walk with them, thereby keeping their attention on what they are doing while they get used to each other's presence.
4. Confine the dogs near each other for a few days (though not *with* each other) so that they can get used to each other's presence.

5. Before you put the dogs together for the first time, take them on a long hike and wear them out so that they will not have pent-up energy, which will add to the chance of confrontation.

Aggression Toward Animals (Non Canines)

People are often upset when they bring a new dog into the home with their existing cats, chickens, birds, or horses, just to have them attempt to kill the existing animals. This is something that needs to be considered before bringing an older dog home. Dogs are by nature predatory animals. Many of the breeds available are bred specifically for high prey drive, since these drives are utilized by humans for hunting, ratting, herding, etc. Because of this, dogs need to be introduced to the animals they will be expected to live with during the time that they are still puppies.

If the dog has high prey drives and cannot be expected to live with prey animals, then the most you can expect is for the dog to be obedience trained well enough that it will maintain a down/stay in the presence of these animals. This means that you must always be present in order to be sure that the prey animals near the dog are safe. When you are not present, the dog should be kept safely away from these animals by using confinement either for the animals or the dog.

It is important to always keep in mind that a dog is a predatory animal by nature. People tend to humanize them and become emotionally involved on a human level. While there is nothing wrong with having a strong emotional attachment to your dog, it is dangerous to humanize them, as applying human logic to an animal is unrealistic. Dogs do have the ability to think, but they lack *complex* reasoning ability. This means that when you are not present the dog is not going to be thinking "I shouldn't chase the horse, because my owner doesn't like for me to do that."

The only way that you can hope to ensure that the dog will not revert to prey chasing behavior in your absence is to continually make certain that the dog gets no benefit from attempts to chase the horse (or prey animal) and always has a negative association with doing so. In order to do this, you must be present and not allow the dog to be rewarded by doing so in your absence. This is a self-rewarding behavior as the dog enjoys the chase and potentially the kill.

Re-Directed Aggression

We once received a frantic call from a lawyer, "Stan," and his wife, "Carol," who lived in the Hollywood Hills. They explained that they had owned a female Rottweiler happily and without incident for six years. The couple then heard about a two year old female of the same breed that had been abandoned and decided to take her on. Their old dog was "Layla," and they named the new dog "Katie." Layla was immediately unhappy with Katie upon meeting her. She growled and snarled, and when the couple yelled at her, she stalked away. One night, the couple had decided to give Katie a bath in their bathtub. Carol was kneeling next to the tub, washing Katie with the bathroom door open. Suddenly, Layla came running into the bathroom and jumped onto Katie's back, savagely attacking her around the head and shoulders. Carol was so surprised that she didn't have a chance to pull her hands away. She was bitten severely during the struggle. Stan said it was literally a blood bath when he entered the bathroom after hearing Carol's screams. He narrowly missed being bitten himself as he grabbed Layla by the collar to pull her off of Katie. Katie and Carol both had to be taken to the emergency room for stitches, and they wondered if they could ever trust Layla again.

This is a classic case of redirected aggression. Think of a bar fight where a man begins to fight with a stranger and when his friend tries to hold him back he punches his friend in the nose. This is because the adrenaline is flowing. The man does not mean to punch his friend, but his body has registered the fight vs. flight instinct and he is temporarily acting on pure instinct. This is why you never want to reach into a dog fight.

It is also not wise to reach out to grab a dog's collar when it is in full aggression mode at a door or fence. The likelihood of redirected aggression is high at these times. When two dogs are fighting you are best off to do one of two things:

1. Grab a hose and hose the dogs down. When you startle them in this way it changes the dogs from fight to flight mode. Their self-protective instincts should kick in and they should jump back from the fight if only giving you a few seconds to break them apart. If necessary you may have to put the hose in the dogs nose or in its mouth so that it has to let go or risk drowning.

2. Grab each dog by the tail or hind legs, lifting them up into the air so only their front feet are on the ground. Without gaining traction they should release out of surprise at the lack of balance. You must back up as fast as you can, keeping them off balance so that you won't get a redirected bite towards your legs.

If you are alone, this is much more difficult to do and should only be attempted if you are (a) experienced with dogs and (b) strong. You will want to choose the most dominant dog, so that when he releases the other dog can get away.

We are not suggesting that you do this if you are alone, as it can be very dangerous. You are much better off allowing the dogs to fight while you get help or stay out of it, as dogs can sometimes fight with minimal damage compared to what they can do to you. Dogs are covered with fur for protection, whereas human skin is much more fragile.

How did things eventually turn out with Layla and Katie? They were both brought in for obedience training and kept side by side in the kennels. Katie had never been trained before, and Layla had been to puppy training five years prior. We established pack leadership rituals with Stan and Carol and had them take the dogs on daily walks together. They were to focus on the exercise and keep the dogs moving, so they didn't have time to deal with each other one on one. After exercising, they practiced the "place" command in the same room on either side of the couch with the owners present. Although they were much improved, they could not be trusted alone together and slept in separate crates, using dog runs periodically so that they could each have their own time to run in the yard. Layla was given more freedom than Katie, as she was older and was accustomed to her freedom. Katie, who had been rescued from a shelter, still had some chewing issues that were being worked out with the confinement conditioning process.

Layla unfortunately died of cancer two years later, and Katie took over the main position in the house. Stan and Carol took our advice and purchased a male puppy, which Katie readily accepted. It had taken awhile for things to work out, but everything turned out well for Stan and Carol.

Boredom Related Aggression

Boredom can add to conflict. Think of your children when they have to stay in the house on a rainy day. The confinement to a small area and the presence of boredom often result in arguments and squabbles between siblings. Similarly, dogs left alone together in a small yard with nothing to occupy their time may begin to squabble. Adding toys and things to chew on may complicate the problem by causing possessiveness issues.

If you are home, the best solution is to exercise the dogs. Dogs that are tired will be much more likely to get along together. If exercise is not possible, temporary separation may be the answer. When you separate dogs, you can more easily provide toys and chew bones for each without possessiveness issues. Using dog runs, they can each have their own shade, shelter, and water. Later, when you return home, you can let them out to play together when possessiveness and boredom are no longer issues.

Frustration-Related Aggression

Without a doubt, one of the foremost contributors to dog aggression is tying the animal out in a yard. Tying a dog creates frustration whenever the dog hits the end of the tether. A high percentage of the dogs that end up on the six o'clock news for biting people have a history of being tied out. There is no need to tie a dog. If the dog jumps fences or escapes the yard, he should be put in a covered dog run. A dog run of the proper size (minimum 5 x 20) allows the dog to move about and relieve itself. It should, as always, also have the basics of food, water, shade, and shelter. Dog runs should be on cement so that the dog cannot dig out, and so that they can be easily cleaned and disinfected. You may certainly make your dog run larger than 5 x 20, provided that you have the space and the concrete to put it on. Dog runs can be very basic, with portable chain link panels or elaborate with wrought iron and potted plants around the exterior to disguise them. There are many different ways that people approach the use of the dog run.

Dog runs should be washed each day and scooped several times per day. There should always be a fresh bucket of water kept in the shade and ample shelter, with at least a basic dog house for the dog to escape from the elements. You will always want to keep the run near the house so that it is easy for you to feed and have access to the dog. Human nature makes it less likely for you to interact with the dog the further away from the house that he is kept.

One of the benefits of using a simple portable chain link run is that you can take it down and move it in a matter of minutes. If you decide to change its location or you are moving, the run is portable and does not have required posts cemented into the ground. Also, keep in mind that you don't want to place the dog in an area where he can constantly see people coming and going, or children playing. This can cause frustration for the dog, which can result in excessive barking, destruction, and even self-mutilation. Privacy fences, lattice, and even vegetation can be an aid to blocking such a view.

Barrier frustration can be the cause of territorial aggression. Another common cause of lawsuits stemming from dog bites is the dog that is kept behind short fences in front yards that border on sidewalks. We have been expert witnesses in more than one court case where this was a factor. Dogs are naturally territorial and even the most social dog kept next to a sidewalk, where it is teased on a regular basis, can become aggressive. The teasing creates a time bomb in the dog, which later erupts when he actually gets a chance to bite someone walking down the sidewalk. If the gate is accidentally left open or the dog manages to leap the fence, then the next person coming down the sidewalk will probably be bitten.

Consider this example: We were expert witnesses in a dog bite case that occurred in Los Angeles. A couple had three untrained Rottweilers in their front yard behind a less than adequate chain link fence that bordered on a sidewalk. The dogs were a one year old male, and his mother and father, who were each a couple of years older than him. None of the dogs had been spayed or neutered. A few of the neighbors knew the dogs well enough to pet them over the fence (a situation that always poses the risk of liability on the owner's part), while others such as the kids and teenagers in the area would tease them as they walked home from school or rode their bicycles past. The front gate latch had been broken and instead of fixing it the owner had propped the gate closed with an old car battery.

In the past, the dogs had produced several litters of puppies, which the neighborhood children had gotten in a habit of stealing. The children would generally distract the adult dogs with food in one corner of the yard, while another child would enter the yard via the gate and grab a puppy and run. This had gone on over the last year on and off and had created a great amount of frustration in the dogs. One fateful Sunday morning, this same scenario played itself out, but when the teenager exited the yard with the stolen puppy, he left the gate wide open. Out came the enraged Rottweilers into the street. At the same time, a little old Korean man was walking down the sidewalk headed for morning services at his church. The dogs attacked the innocent man and dragged him into the street. He screamed for help, but nobody in the neighborhood was brave enough to come to his aid. He was dragged around the street by his arms and his legs for twenty minutes until a policeman arrived and saved him by hitting the dogs in the head with the butt of his shotgun. The dogs then gave up the attack and ran back into their front yard.

After the man was taken to the hospital, it was determined that he had lost a pint of blood from the attack. The victim won his case for two million dollars against both the owners and the landlords for keeping the dogs in unsafe conditions. This is a prime example of how frustration can turn to aggression given the right set of circumstances.

In this case, the dogs' frustration level had built up over time. Their natural territorial nature was heightened by their puppies being stolen. The bite evidence showed a series of punctures meant to inflict harm and drive the perpetrator (in the dog's minds) away. These were wounds that showed that the intent of the dogs was to defend territory, not to catch and possess prey. Prey wounds would have been large tears and, because the man was prone on the ground for a long time, would have resulted in death by an attack on the man's exposed neck. The dogs had every opportunity to kill the man, but to the learned observer it was obvious that the dogs were in defense mode. They were biting and releasing in order to drive the man out of their area. The releases were meant to give the man an opportunity to flee or move back away from the territory. This was in no way a legal defense for the owner, but it did illustrate the mindset of the dogs. This case is a prime example of how *not* to manage your dogs.

Negligence and Abuse

The previous case is a good example of negligence on the owner's part. Abuse is yet another situation that can create a dangerous dog. It is an old assumption that dangerous dogs are always a product of abuse. While this certainly can be the case, the previous examples should show you that there are many causes for aggression in dogs and diagnosis can be difficult.

Abuse comes in many forms and rehabilitation of the abused dog will depend on whether you can get it out of abusive hands, as well as whether the dog is genetically sound to begin with. The hardest dog to rehabilitate is the one who has weak nerves and has been abused in addition to this.

Like children of abuse, dogs who grow up being abused can become abusers themselves. It is quite common for abused dogs to cower towards their owners but then turn aggressive to the children in the house and those less able to defend themselves, such as weaker dogs or puppies. It is very sad to see a dog in this situation that is put down for biting a child. The dog's death in this case is simply a byproduct of its environment.

We saw this unfairness play out in the case of an American Bulldog named "Jake." He was brought to us because he had been snapping at the children in the family. It turned out that the reasons were twofold. He had a tooth that was broken down to the root and infected, and whenever he had sought attention by jumping up on the owners they had kicked and hit at him and screamed "down." Due to this reaction, he would bolt, bite, and scratch at the owners whenever he was given the Down Command. He had made an association between the word "Down" and an all out assault on him by the owners. In this case, the owners were willing to see the error of their ways and began to work with us to fix both the dog's teeth and its wounded spirit.

In yet another case of abuse we were called by a breeder friend to help train a young German Shepherd Dog from one of her breedings. She explained that the dog was acting out aggressively to the owner and visitors. She stated that she couldn't understand why this would be, as he was well bred and didn't have any genetic propensity to be overly aggressive. She stated that the dog was owned by her secretary and her husband, but they were divorcing so the husband would bring the dog in.

When the husband walked into the consultation room, the first thing that struck us was that he was wearing black leather gloves. When we asked him if there was a reason for the gloves, he said that it was in case the dog tried to bite him. The dog was a beautiful male German Shepherd Dog with dark pigment and intelligent eyes. During the consultation, the man showed no affection toward the dog, but the dog was highly responsive to our testing, and although not completely trusting, he showed no sign of offensive or defensive aggression. Because the dog owner described the dog, "Alex," as being willing to bite him "out of the blue," we had to wonder if we were looking at Rage

Syndrome. We took him on for training and soon noticed that he showed a marked preference for women over men. He bonded with only two people in my office, myself and my assistant. I could see that he was looking at us as an anchor in the storm, and my heart went out to him. I sensed that there was something more to the story that the owners were leaving out.

A couple of weeks into Alex's training, I received another call from his breeder. She said that she had more information for me. It seemed that since her assistant had filed for divorce from her husband she had begun to open up about the abuse that had been taking place in the house to both her and the dog. The husband apparently drank heavily and became mean. She had told the breeder stories of terrible abuse where the dog was burned intentionally with cigarettes. His tail was pulled and stepped on intentionally. In these episodes he would hit both the woman and the dog with his fist. One day he raised his hand to the dog, and Alex bit him. This was the reason for the gloves.

I was saddened that I would eventually have to give Alex back to his abusive owner. The wife had moved into an apartment where she could not keep him, and she didn't have the stomach to fight with him over the dog. The breeder suggested that I try to purchase the dog from the owner since he was already afraid of Alex. I did in fact make this offer as I felt that because of the dog's strong genetic background he could be totally rehabilitated. The man was in fact about to accept my offer when the breeder made the mistake of calling him, urging him to accept. At this time, he wrongfully made the assumption that I was in cahoots with his wife, whom I had never met or even spoken to on the phone. He came and picked up the dog out of anger and never took one lesson with him. Alex disappeared forever back into the hands of his abuser.

Jealousy

Dogs have the same set of emotions as young children. We all know how jealous children can be of other children with toys that they covet or with their parents' attention. Likewise, dogs have many of the same issues.

Take Shawna for example, a client who was a first time mother. She called us for help because her Old English Sheep Dog was trying to attack her baby anytime it crawled near her sliding glass door. The dog, who had been banished to the backyard since the baby was born, would go into a frothing rage whenever it saw the child. Shawna needed help, or she was going to get rid of the dog.

Upon interviewing her, we found that she had purchased her dog as a puppy, approximately a year before she became pregnant with her child. The puppy, in her own words, was "my baby." She had worked from home and spent many hours with the puppy in the house and on long walks. She had never formally trained her but had established a very close bond with her. When she became pregnant, she began spending less time with "Daisy" as her belly grew and it became uncomfortable for Daisy to jump on her. Gradually the dog was no longer allowed in the house, and eventually she was literally on the outside looking in. When the baby came, the dog would watch the couple feed the baby and give it attention through the back door. Jealousy grew until the dog began to erupt with full aggression toward the baby anytime it crawled near the back door.

The couple really had no idea why Daisy was acting the way she was until we pointed out the error of their ways. The solution was basic obedience and teaching ritual behaviors (stopping at doors, gates, and boundaries, and the "place" command) because in doing so the owners were spending quality time with Daisy, while teaching her at the same time that they were in control. Next came the process of lessening the animosity toward the baby. We did this after basic obedience was established by sending them on long walks together with one of them pushing the stroller and the other making the dog Heel alongside. By keeping them moving, Daisy got used to the presence of the baby without facing off with him. We then gradually started a nightly ritual where the parents would hold the baby on the couch and have Daisy present on the leash, giving her attention at the same time. The parents would trade off the responsibilities with who had the baby and who had Daisy. They gradually worked their way to doing this while sitting side by side. In addition, Daisy was brought into the house in her crate, where she could safely observe all of the goings on in the house without endangering the baby. Any hostility at all while she was in the crate would result in a stream of vinegar and water in the nose accompanied by a harsh "No." This only occurred on a couple of occasions in the beginning, and then it never happened again. Daisy seemed to be content to just be included in the house. When the baby was asleep in its crib, the couple would bring her out in the Place Command so that she was the center of attention in the evenings or at nap time, when the baby was not present. These changes worked well. The couple was cautioned never to leave the baby alone with the dog, as even without a prior history of aggression, dogs tend to think that they can correct children in the owners' absence. This goes back to their pack mentality.

Territorial Aggression

Many owners overlook the importance of territory to dogs. Even a dog that is not normally aggressive to strangers might be when the stranger enters their home or territory. This is a natural instinct for canines. Wolves and wild dogs stake out large blocks of territory that they aggressively defend. This is one trait that attracted man to living with dogs originally, as they act as an alarm system and defender.

People often walk their dogs down the street that they live on, allowing them to mark territory along the way. This may have the effect of naturally expanding the dogs territory in its mind beyond its own yard. A frustration can begin to build for the extremely territorial dog, as he may return to find that another dog in the neighborhood may have marked over his scent marker. This may cause enough tension in the dog for him to begin to attempt to escape the yard for territorial marking purposes. This also contributes to his desire to fight with other dogs in the neighborhood and even bite strangers as they walk in the neighborhood due to the fact that in his mind they are encroaching upon his territory.

The best advice that we can give to the owner of a highly territorial dog, or one who has become obsessed with escaping the yard to mark territory, is to walk the dog elsewhere. If you put the dog in the car and drive a distance before you walk, he will not be extending his territory in the immediate neighborhood.

Owner Protection

Many dogs are overly protective of their owners. We see this at our facility quite often. A dog may be unapproachable when being held by its owner, but after being separated from them, the dog then becomes calm and easy to handle. This is generally the result of owner passivity. The dog takes on the Alpha role because the owner seems to support this behavior by making the mistake of stroking the dog while it is being aggressive, thereby supporting the aggression. The dog usually has a history of being the

Alpha at home as well, and therefore protection of the owner is a natural progression when away from home as well.

Owner protection can only be solved by the owner being willing to step up and take charge of the situation. Obedience training and establishing ritual behaviors around the house are critical to success in these situations. There is a conflict in the mind of many owners in this situation, and many will say "but I want him to protect me if I need him to."

It is important that the owner understands that a trained protection dog or police dog has obedience training and is taught to respond aggressively *on command*.

The owner needs to understand that when a dog decides to respond aggressively on his own without a control command, there is a high likelihood of an unprovoked bite, which can result in a lawsuit. This situation is dangerous and embarrassing. The odds are in fact much more in favor of this type of situation than an actual attack on the owner. If the owner is that concerned about being attacked by a perpetrator, then they should extend the dog's training to protection after finishing obedience training rather than continuing to let the dog be a danger to the public.

Another common mistake people make with their dogs is to greet visitors at the door with the dog. This has the effect of making the dog think about a confrontation. From the dog's point of view the knock on the door or the ringing of the doorbell signals an intruder in the territory. If the dog is the least bit defensive or territorial, his adrenaline begins to flow much like Pavlov's dog would salivate because the ringing of a bell signified food. This becomes a conditioned reaction. The chances of an aggressive response from the dog at the door are increased ten-fold due to the adrenaline and the confrontation at the door. If you simply substitute a different ritual that works for you, such as the dog being sent to Place when the doorbell rings, the dog learns that the doorbell means time to Place in a relaxed down stay. The guest can then enter the home and the dog can calm down before introductions are made. This simple ritual keeps the dog knowing that the owner is in control and allows the adrenaline to diminish prior to contact with the guest.

There are some dogs that are so territorial and high in defense that the best solution for them is not to allow them to be near guests in the first place. The owners need to ask themselves what can be gained versus what can be lost if they allow the dog to interact with company. In most states the law dictates that an invited guest has the right to expect you to have a safe environment for them to enter. It is a reasonable assumption for them to expect not to be attacked by your dog when they enter.

The Law and Dog Bites
If your dog bites an invited guest in your home, whether it be a repair person or friend, you are strictly liable. If, however, the dog bites an *intruder* in your home (not outside) you are not liable. Outside of your home legal standards are usually less transparent. These circumstances often have to be worked out in a court of law.

It is, for instance, different if your dog bites a twenty-six year old man who jumped your fence than it is if he bites a thirteen year old boy who was retrieving his baseball. Different questions then come into play, including whether or not you had signs posted, whether you had warned the boy to stay out of your yard, or whether he had a reasonable expectation of being safe in your yard because you often invited him in.

There was a case a few years ago in Palm Springs, California, where two Rottweilers killed an intruder that broke into their home while the owners were away at work. Apparently the dogs had been sleeping by the side of the house unbeknownst to the intruder. He entered the home through the kitchen window. The dogs woke up and followed the intruder into the house by jumping through the open window. The owners came home to find the intruder dead on the bathroom floor with a single mattress on top of him. He had apparently grabbed it as a shield in an attempt to fend off the dogs' bites. He had over thirty bite wounds on his body and had bled out on the bathroom floor. The dogs were initially taken away by animal control, which is when we received a call with a request to defend them. They were soon released back to their owners and no charges were filed. The police told us that in their opinion the dogs were just doing their job. At the autopsy the man was found to have overdosed on drugs and had a heart attack during the attack. In any case, the dogs were within their rights to attack the intruder inside of their home.

In the eyes of the law this is no different than if you shot an intruder who entered your home. It would be considered self-defense. It is a different situation all together if you were to shoot someone in defense of your property while they were in your yard. You are only allowed to use deadly force when you, or another person, have a reasonable fear for your life. This is the same for the use of a dog. A person who breaks and enters into your home has no reasonable expectation of safety. An invited guest does.

The law also states that the public has a reasonable expectation for you to keep them safe from your dog. This means that if your dog bites someone out in public, you are strictly liable with an exception if the person bitten was physically assaulting you or attempting to do so.

If a purse snatcher grabs your purse while you have your dog on a leash and the dog bites him in response to his physical assault on you, the dog's action is considered reasonable. You cannot, however, send your dog on a chase after him to apprehend him, because at that point you are not under direct physical threat.

If your dog is off of his leash and away from your property when he bites someone, you are completely out of luck unless you were being assaulted or protecting someone else from assault where their life was in danger. At that point, you better hope that there are witnesses. Many states have leash laws that make you strictly liable if your dog causes harm to someone while not on a leash. At this point, the law is clear that you have already violated one law prior to the bite. You can even be sued if your dog runs into the street and causes a car accident or scares someone by running up to them and causes them to fall down in fear. Dog bites are not the only way that your dog can get you in trouble.

Conclusion

The best way to prevent your dog from getting you into legal trouble is:

1. Select your dog carefully for temperament and trainability, and research your breeds prior to your selection.

2. Train the dog professionally and thoroughly when it is young, keeping up ritual behaviors that keep you in charge.

3. Contain your dog behind proper fencing, whether it be a dog run on cement or behind sturdy fencing with locked gates, away from public traffic areas. *Never tie the dog out.* The only exception to this is when he is on a place command in a relaxed down stay, directly with you, where he is not hitting the end of the leash. This can be an extra precaution if you are camping or out in the front yard washing your car. The dog should never be left alone in this circumstance.

1. Never have the dog off leash in a public place. If your dog is known to be aggressive to strangers, teach him to wear a muzzle in public.

2. Use the rule "When in doubt, don't" as it applies to decisions you make when introducing your dog to strangers or having him loose around invited guests.

3. Never force your dog on people who are not comfortable around dogs. Respect other people's feelings and put the dog away in an appropriate place. If the dog's behavior worries you in any way, seek professional help.

XI. TRAVELING WITH YOUR CANINE COMPANION

The dog backpack allows you to take all of the possessions the dog may need on a road trip and carry them on his back so that you wont have to carry them.

Traveling with your dog can be a fun and rewarding experience. Going places where you can hike together, play in rivers, or swim in the ocean create fond memories. There are, however, certain things that you should do when traveling with your dog that make life easier and much more comfortable for both of you.

Crates

Crates, when used properly, should not be seen or referred to as "cages." They serve as a traveling bed for your dog. If properly sized, your dog should be able to stand up, turn around, and lay down in it. We suggest the use of the heavy duty plastic type for traveling for several reasons. This type of crate is easy to clean, keeps all dirt, hair, sand etc. inside, and if your dog should get sick, it will be much easier to clean and keep your car clean than the wire versions. The plastic crates also create shade from the sun and shelter from the rain if you should find yourself in the elements.

The crate is the safest place for the dog to be if you are camping and you need to have your hands free to cook or do other chores. He can lie down comfortably in his crate under a shade tree or in the tent. This also keeps him safe from other animals, such as bears, that might wander into your campsite.

Transporting a dog using the crate is the safest way for him to ride. That way if you are involved in an accident, he will not become a projectile flying through your car. Crates held in place by bungee cords are much safer in the rear bed of a truck than having the dog tied to a rope. In case of an accident, the dog will not be thrown around or hung because he is not tied by the neck.

Over the years, we have known several people who have been in accidents with their dogs in the car. In one case, a breeder friend of ours was in an accident on the freeway, where her van flipped upside down. She had six English Mastiffs with her at the time, but because they were all in crates they all survived without injury.

Another benefit that the crate provides is keeping dogs separate when you are attending an event such as a dog show or if you are hunting with multiple dogs and handlers. This allows people to be less stressed, as they can get their dogs out and put them away at their leisure, and they don't have to stand around holding them by their leashes all the time.

Do not Leave Your Dog in a Hot Vehicle
The rule of thumb is that if you cannot stay in the vehicle without the air-conditioning on, your dog can't either. One of the most ignorant statements we hear from time to time is" He is a dog; he can handle more than people can!"Wrong! Dogs do not have the ability to sweat like people do. They have to pant to regulate their body temperature. In addition, they have a fur coat on and generally can handle cold a lot

better than heat. The exception to this is dogs lacking undercoats. For a dog, being left in a hot car is a lot like you being in the same car with a winter coat on. When in doubt, don't! Either leave the air conditioning on, don't stop in the first place, or take the dog with you when you leave the car.

Crates and Hotel Rooms

Hotels that allow dogs in the rooms really appreciate it when their owners bring crates along. To the hotel owner, the crate means that the dog will most likely not damage the hotel room. They know that dogs left in unfamiliar places can panic and cause quite a bit of damage. Having a crate provides the dog with familiar surroundings and keeps him from exploring his new location. When the weather outside is too hot or cold to allow the dog to stay in the car while the owner goes to dinner, the dog can stay safe and comfortable in the room without danger of destruction. A television or radio left on at this time also serves to make the dog more comfortable and masks sounds that otherwise might make him nervous.

Crates and Airplanes

If you don't have to fly with your dog, then you are better off not to. We say this after years of experience flying with dogs. Flying can be very traumatic for a dog. The dog has to be handled in the crate by people he doesn't know. Some of these people are kind and considerate of the dogs needs, but others are indifferent and some can even be cruel. The dog has to be loaded with the luggage, and there is nothing an owner can do if a careless baggage attendant throws that crate or lets it fall off of the conveyer belt. We have seen this happen. We know people who have gone to the trouble of getting their dogs Therapy Dog Certifications just in order to be able to fly with him in the passenger compartment. You can hardly blame these people for going the extra mile as there have been numerous animal deaths caused by airlines who failed to pressurize the areas where the dogs were kept, or let the dogs perish from heat exhaustion or cold.

With the cost of sending the dog in the crate you might as well just buy him a seat. If you qualify to take your dog on board, it is a good idea to bring a blanket to put under the dog on the seat. This way there will not be any hair left over for the next person to worry about when you get off the plane. You should always check with the airline for their various requirements regarding flying with dogs, as they vary greatly between airlines. The aforementioned plastic crates are the only type that the airline will allow apart from some forms of metal crates, which weigh more and thus will cost more to ship. The crates must have proper stickers, with owner contact information affixed, as well as required food and water cups. Water is necessary for the dog, but will obviously spill in transportation. Our recommendation is to freeze water into the plastic cup provided with the crate the night before. This way it will melt gradually and provide the dog with water periodically throughout the day. We do not recommend food unless your shipping is going to require an overnight stay. If so, the food should be attached in a zip-lock container and measured out correctly.

When an overnight stay is required, the dog may be sent to a temporary boarding facility at the airport location. This only happens if a mistake is made and the dog ends up somewhere that it shouldn't have been sent, or if the owners do not arrive to pick up the dog. While it sounds unlikely, it has happened to us. Coming back from Europe with two dogs in tow, we had a layover in Minnesota. There were freezing temperatures at the time, and the airline told us that we would have to spend the night and hope that it was warm enough to fly with the dogs in the morning. We spent the night in a hotel after being assured that the dogs would be taken to a nearby kennel. We even double and triple checked to make sure that the dogs would be cared for properly. Upon arriving the next morning, we were told that it was warm enough to fly and that we were booked on the next flight. We waited, and our dogs never arrived. We finally got a straight answer just before the flight left that our dogs had been mistakenly put on the flight the night before even though it was too cold to fly them. Luckily they were alive in Los Angeles, but they had to spend the night at a boarding kennel there due to the fact that we were still in Minneapolis.

Another suggestion when traveling on an airline with a crated dog is to put florescent tape on top of your crate. Since there are sometimes multiple people flying with dogs, you can tell from the passenger compartment of the plane just which crate is yours. We also drill holes in the sides of the doorways in our crates and fasten the gate closed with zip ties. This way someone won't accidentally let your dog out.

Years ago an associate trainer of ours from France had a well-meaning but ignorant airline employee let his dog out of the crate to give him a drink of water. The dog ran away and out onto the tarmac at O'Hare airport. Despite knowing that his dog was loose, the airline let him take off, leaving his dog behind. It took a week for someone in the Chicago area to find him (only because it was on the nightly news for a week), and by then the dog was starving and had been hit by a car. He was missing teeth and had scrapes on his legs. Those little zip ties could have saved him a lot of grief.

Travel Kits For Dogs

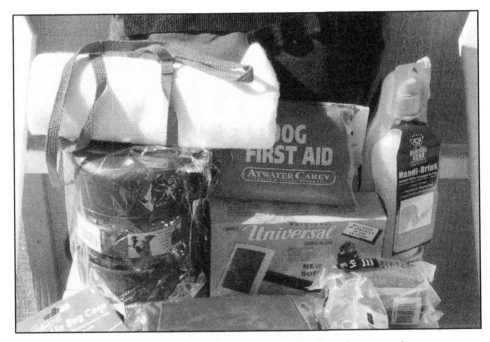

Items that you should always have on hand in the dogs pack are: First Aid Kit, Brush, Bottle of Water, Container of Food, Water and Food Dish, Towel, Hasty leash, Waste Pick Up Bags, Bandages, Clean up Wipes, Medicines.

If you are going to travel with a dog, you should carry a travel kit that includes essentials for the dog. A small day pack is good for this purpose. If you are going to hike with your dog, you may want to provide him with his own backpack. There are simple backpacks for day hikes and more elaborate backpacks for journeys that take several days. Simple backpacks usually have basic nylon straps and are manufactured to carry a basic amount of weight. Backpacks made for long treks will have sheepskin lining the nylon in order to prevent rubbing the dog and will be manufactured to carry more weight. Some of the things that should be contained in the pack are:

1. A water bottle and a light-weight, collapsible water dish.
2. Food Container and collapsible food dish and/or power bars for dogs.
3. Appropriate brush for his coat type.
4. Basic First Aid supplies in case of injury.
5. Paw protection and eye protection.
6. Towel to dry him off if he gets wet.
7. Sanitary Bags (for proper public area etiquette).

From these basics, you can add whatever might be appropriate for the setting you will be in. If you are going to be in a boat, you may want to bring a canine life preserver. If you are playing at the park, you may want to include a Frisbee or some toys. A cool pack might be appropriate for a desert trip and so on.

Canine Car Seats and Harnesses

If you don't have room in your vehicle for a crate, you might consider a canine car seat or safety harness. This is like a child seat for a dog. There are many different types of seats and car harnesses dependent on the size of the dog that you have.

The bottom line is that you should find a method that suits you, so that the dog doesn't get hurt or hurt you or your family members should you be involved in an accident. All of these safety devices also offer the added benefit that your dog cannot jump out of the vehicle as soon as you open the door.

Vehicle Ramp

In your dog's life, there will eventually come a time where he cannot or should not jump into your vehicle, such as after surgeries or when he gets older and suffers from joint pain.

Owners' physical conditions often come into play here as well. Owners of large dogs that have physical limitations of their own can often strain their backs trying to lift dogs of well over one-hundred pounds into a vehicle.

A dog ramp is the perfect solution for this problem. These ramps can be folded in half and stored in your SUV or van. They unfold in seconds and are light weight, yet sturdy.

Eye and Foot Protection

Eye protection is recommended for dogs if they are going to stick their heads out of windows while driving or while boating, or where there may be blowing sand.

Don't forget to protect your dog's eyes and feet from the elements. A dog's eyes can be protected from UV rays just as ours can. Dog Goggles will protect his eyes from blowing wind and sand, so that if he wants to stick his head out the window it won't hurt him. There are many types and styles to fit any breed.

A dog's feet can be harmed by glass, frost, and burning asphalt. There are many types of booties that protect the feet. Some are made for foul weather, such as snow and rain, others are more fashionable but still protect from heat and debris. You should always look for the booties that have a fastener around the ankle so that they stay on well.

Discover Locations That Allow Dogs

There are various businesses, restaurants, and hotels across the country that allow dogs, many of which outright cater to them. You can now locate these facilities with the help of books, magazines, and the internet. For example try: www.DogFriendly.com or www.FidoFriendly.com, or check out your local book store or Amazon. com for books that cover the areas you will be visiting.

XII. COLLEGE FOR DOGS (TITLES AND CERTIFICATIONS)

Dogs, like humans, can receive degrees, awards, and certifications. They cannot however, do this without your help and dedication.

Just as college requires passing one's high school courses, it is a pre-requisite for most titles and certifications that a dog has accomplished his basic obedience. There are some exceptions to this as with conformation (beauty) competitions and dog games (such as flyball or dock diving), but even fun and games will benefit from the communications skills provided by obedience.

The following are some of the titles and certifications that you might consider pursuing with your dog. Some of them are simply recreational, while others are very serious undertakings, such as Search and Rescue, where you train to save lives.

Since many of these categories would require their own book to thoroughly articulate the training process, we have supplied current web sites with more information, as well as books listed in the Recommended Reading section.

American Kennel Club (AKC)
The American Kennel Club is the premier dog club in the United States of America. Established in 1884, the American Kennel Club originally followed English precedents of show structure. Eventually, the

American Kennel Club established itself as a uniquely American organization.

Today, the AKC offers many different titles and sports competitions from conformation shows (beauty titles), where dogs can obtain a Championship as a true representative of their breed's structure, to working titles that are based solely on the dogs working performance in their respective breed classifications.

The following is the web site for further information on the American Kennel Club and the Rules and Regulations for various events that this organization offers to its members: www.AKC.org.

Click on the Events portion of the web site to find the certification that you are interested in. The following are brief synopses of what you will find there:

Agility

This is a fast-paced and exciting sport, which is both fun for you and the dog and entertaining for spectators. The sport is open to all breeds recognized by the AKC, and the only aspect of the sport that is changed by breed is the height of the jumps and the time in which the dog is expected to run the course. There

are two types of agility classes. The first is the Standard Class, which includes obstacle work such as the A-frame, Dog walk, and the seesaw. The second class is jumpers and weavers, which includes the jumps and the weave poles. Both classes offer various levels such as Novice, Open, Excellent and Masters Titles.

After completing both of the classes with a ranking of "Excellent," the team may compete in the MACH (Masters Agility Champion Title). Other web sites related to agility outside of the AKC:
Dogs On Course: www.docna.com
Established in 2005

Canine Performance Events: www.K9cpe.com
CPE's basic philosophy is for the dog and owner to have fun.

United States Dog Agility Association: www.usdaa.com
Promoting Competitive Excellence in Dog Agility

Canine Good Citizen (CGC)

Before taking the CGC test (Canine Good Citizen), owners must sign a pledge to agree to be a responsible dog owner. This includes taking care of their dog's health needs, safety, and training. The owners also pledge to clean up after their dogs in public and not to allow them to infringe on the rights of others.

The tests involve accepting a friendly stranger, sitting politely while being petted, appearance and grooming, walking on a loose lead, walking through a crowd, obeying sit and down stay commands, coming when called, reaction to distraction, and supervised separation. Encouragement is allowed throughout the test.

Many dog owners choose to become introduced to the AKC events by obtaining a CGC, which is a pass or fail test. The CGC should not be confused with an obedience title. This is a test for dog owners to show that their dogs can behave in public and be good citizens. Many countries have adopted similar programs, which may be carried out in various forms. One such link is provided below:

The Canadian equivalent of the CGC is the CCGCT or Canadian Canine Good Citizen Test tm. This test must be taken in a busy public place, such as a shopping mall, hotel or community center. This test is not to be conducted in a regular training atmosphere. This program embraces both purebred and mixed breed dogs.
For more information: www.habac.ca/ccgct.htm

Conformation (Breed Championships)
Conformation shows are the beauty pageants of dog shows and are the signature event for the AKC. Each dog breed is judged according to the breed standards set forth by the parent breed club (or main organization for the breed in the United States). The dog is judged on proper appearance for the breed, including height, weight, proportion, coat, color, correctness of type, and movement. Temperament is judged to the degree that it is obvious to the judge while being presented.

There are two standards for the dogs being judged. The dog must be of basic breed standard and without obvious disqualifying faults in order to be allowed in the class to be judged. The second standard is that of Champion quality, which is based on the judge's opinion. The proper amount of points must be obtained over several shows under multiple judges for a dog to be recognized as a Champion.

For more information on conformation shows in various parts of the world contact your local breed club for standards. Below is a link to provide some extra information: www.answers.com/topic/conformation-show

Coonhound Events

As of 2005, the AKC is offering a brand new Coonhound event, with titles of Nite Champion, Grand Nite Champion, and Supreme Nite Champion. Bench shows, field trials, nite hunts, and water races will all be allowed to show the prowess of the coonhound. For more information on the new AKC trials go to: www.akccoonhounds.org

Earthdog Tests

Earthdogs are typically Terriers and Dachshunds that have the natural "go to ground" instincts in chasing small vermin. The behaviors tested are: willingness to follow scent to an entrance, willingness to enter a dark den, and willingness to work the quarry. This willingness is judged on caged vermin, and the judge evaluates the aggression, lunging, digging, growling, and biting toward the protective bars on the cage.

For more information on Earthdogs and trials both in the United States, Canada, Great Britain, and Australia, go to: www.K9web.com/dog-faqs/activities/earthdogs.html. Here you will find an explanation of Earthdogs, their history, trials, and The American Working Terrier Association (AWTA) www.dirt-dog.com/awta/index.cfm

Other links:
www.dogantics.com/welshiepup/earthdog.shtml
www.duffyscavern.corg/new_to_the_earth.htm
www.terrierman.com/tunneltips.com

Field Trials

Field Trials are open to Basset Hounds, Beagles, Dachshunds, Pointing Breeds, Retrievers, and Spaniels. Each of these tests is different based upon the breed of dog and the type of hunting skills the breed should display. There are many different field trials available in the United States.

Additional information is available on these sites:
www.veterinarypartner.com
Beagle, Bassett Hound, and Dachshund Field Trials
www.beaglesunlimited.net/ftclubs.htm
Everything you want to know about field trials for Beagles www.myoan.net/shootingart/fieldtrials.htm
Describes Field Trials for all eligible breeds

Hunting Trials

Hunting Trials are open to Pointing Breeds, Retrievers, and Spaniels and vary based on the skills that the breed was designed to accomplish. For more information on Field Trials and Hunting Trials and each of the Rules and Regulations go to: www.AKC.org/events/index.cfm
Additional information on Hunting Trials can be found on: www.spanielsinthefield.com

#1 rated Google site for flushing Spaniels. Offers all information regarding this sport, including magazines, rules, events, organizations, clubs, medical information pertaining to the breeds, and recipes for the game birds.

www.nahranews.org

NAHRA - North American Hunting Retriever Association Education for the public in the use of purebred hunting retrievers

www.birddogfoundation.com

National Bird Dog and Retriever Museum-Field Trial Hall of Fame

Herding

Herding tests are open to herding breeds such as the Rottweiler, Standard and Giant Schnauzer, Pyrenean Shepherd, Swedish Valhund, and Greater Swiss Mountain Dog, among others. The Herding Test begins with an instinct test and then goes on to add on more complicated behaviors that incorporate more and more obedience to the handler in fetching sheep, holding, and driving.

Additional information can be found on:

www.AKC.org/events/index.cfm

www.herdingontheweb.com/dogs.htm

Organizations, recourses, all herding breeds, how to start.

Lure Coursing

Lure Coursing is an event set up for Sight Hounds such as Afghans, Basenjis, Rhodesian Ridgebacks, Whippets, and Deerhounds among others. This test is fun for the dogs and keeps them in premium shape while doing something that they love. The lure is set on a pulley device that speeds it along the course. The lure is not an animal, but rather an object, such as a plastic bag. The dogs must give chase by sight and attempt to catch the lure.

www.AKC.org/events/index.cfm

www.asfa.org/coursing.htm

Lure Coursing

The American Sight Hound Field Association. The Sport of Lure Coursing. Very nice site that describes the sport with photos and explains judging criteria.
www.mahahounds.org/coursinginfo.htm

Coursing Info. Explains how to get started and gives some practical tips for novices who are interested in learning about and participating in the sport.

Working Dog Sport
Working Dog Sport is brand new for the AKC as of the date of this publication but has been around for about three decades in America as a strictly European Sport called Schutzhund. This is a sport for working breeds such as the German Shepherd, Rottweiler, and Doberman Pincher among others, which tests the abilities of the dogs for police and guardian work. The new AKC titles will involve obedience, tracking, and protection in the same form as a Schutzhund title (see Schutzhund) but with the new American Kennel Club recognized titles of WD I-III as apposed to the Schutzhund I-III.
See: www.AKC.org/events/index.cfm

Obedience Trials

AKC Obedience Trials offer tests in obedience that range from Novice (Basic On and Off Leash Obedience) Companion Dog to Open (Advanced Obedience and Agility) Companion Dog Excellent, to Utility (Directed Advanced Obedience, Agility, and Scent Discrimination) Dog Titles. Each score in every class must be at least 50% of the exercises with a score of at least 170 out of 200. Each qualifying score is called one leg. It takes three legs under three different judges to achieve a title. The AKC also offers a VCD title for dogs that have achieved Obedience, Agility, and Tracking Titles.

www.AKC.org/events/index.cfm
www.canismajor.com/dog/cdxtitle.html
Nice site that explains obedience titles
www.cesky.org/obedience.htm

A site for Terriers that explains the obedience titles that apply to all breeds offered by the AKC.

AKC Rally

Rally is a fairly new obedience competition for the AKC that bridges the gap between the CGC and the standard Novice, Open, and Utility classes in obedience trials.

In Rally, dogs can receive multiple commands and encouragement from handlers. The style of Rally is more free form, and the handlers do not have to hold their arms in any particular position and may give multiple commands.

www.AKC.org/events/index.cfm

www.canismajor.com/dog/rallyo.html

A nice site that describes Rally in more detail with photos.

Tracking

Tracking tests determine the dog's ability to follow human scent. This is a task that is very useful to man. Each tracking test is more difficult in the number of turns and the age of the track followed.

There are three levels of tracking: TD (Tracking Dog), beginning with a 440 yard track; TDX (Tracking Dog Excellent), 800 to 1000 yard test with an age of 3-5 hours; and VST (Variable Surface Tracking), which includes tracking on surfaces such as vegetation, sand, cement, rain, or snow conditions. When the dog completes all of these he can receive the title of CT (Champion Tracker).

www AKC.org/events/index.cfm

Since tracking is natural for all dogs, it is open to all breeds to compete. For more information you can look at the following sites:
www.dogsnsw.org.au/obedience-and-tracking

A very descriptive site about obedience and tracking testing available through the AKC.
www.proplan.com/sportingdogs/articles/tracking%20test_04.htm
An excellent site to learn how the dog's nose works

UKC (United Kennel Club)

Established in 1898, the United Kennel Club is the largest all breed performance-dog registry in the world. The UKC registers dogs from the Untied States as well as 25 foreign countries. More than 60% of its 12,000 annual licensed events are tests of hunting ability, training and instinct.
www.UKCdogs.com
Events:
Agility
Conformation
Dog Sport
Obedience
Terrier Racing
Weight Pulling

These are just some of the events that the UKC offers. For more information visit the web site listed above. The UKC's events are structured differently and have different rules than the AKC. You should request a Rule Book for any event that you care to consider competing in.

ARBA (American Rare Breed Association)
The mandate of the American Rare Breed Association is to promote and educate the public about the 130 or more breeds from around the world that the American Kennel Club does not yet recognize.
www.arba.org

Dog Sports
Schutzhund
Schutzhund is a sport that originated in Germany as a test for working German Shepherds as police service dogs. It has since become a dog sport that is practiced in a variety of countries around the world. The Schutzhund levels of I-III involve obedience, tracking, and protection exercises with increasing levels of difficulty.
For more information visit:
www.germanshepherddog.com
The site of Schutzhund USA
IPO (The International Version of Schutzhund for All Breeds)

French Ring Sport

French Ring Sport is arguably the most difficult dog sport in the world. It combines the disciplines of Obedience, Agility, and Protection. At the lowest level of training (The Brevet), the dog must walk backwards at the heel and protect its owner from attack while being completely under control.

For more information visit:
www.ringsport.org

Belgian Ring Sport

Belgian Ring Sport is similar to French Ring Sport but far less visible in the United States. This combines Obedience, Agility, and Protection in the same way the French Sport does, but puts the emphasis more on power than on finesse.
www.users.skynet.be/hexental/belringsport.html
Explanation of the origins of Belgian Ring Sport
www.nvbk.org
The Belgian Ring Site in Belgium.

KNPV (Royal Dutch Police Dog)

KNPV is one of the most sought after titles in the world for buyers who wish to purchase a hardcore, intense police dog that has passed tests that are above and beyond what the typical police officer would need from a dog. The tests include retrieving through water, apprehending a person riding a bicycle, and guarding evidence, among others.

For more information see:
www.mc.net/~jimengel/jimread/knpv.htm
www.leerburg.com/knpv

Mondio Ring Sport

Mondio Ring is a place where all of the participants in the various sports above can compete together for a world ring title. There are 17 exercises, which last approximately 45 minutes and include Obedience, Agility, and Protection.
The dogs are worked off-collar and off-leash, and the emphasis is put on control.

For more information visit:
www.usmondioring.corg

Search and Rescue Dogs (SAR)

Search and Rescue dogs are used in disasters such as avalanches, missing persons cases, and water disasters, in addition to use for tracking, trailing, and air scenting scenarios. When the mission turns from Search and Rescue to Search and Recovery, cadaver dogs are used to find the bodies of those who went missing.

For more information see:
www.sardogs.nl
Search and Rescue training in the Netherlands
www.workdogs.com
Describes the various training necessary for Search and Rescue Dogs

Detection Dogs (Narcotics, Explosives, Contraband)

Dogs are used by the military, law enforcement, and security officers to detect illegal substances, explosives, and contraband that ranges from fruits and vegetables to money coming into the country illegally from foreign sources.

For more information see:
www.policek9.com

Information on various police departments using K-9s around the country with links to their sites.
www.doginfomat.com
Information on various types of detection dogs used by law enforcement around the country with links to their sites.

Therapy Dogs

These dogs are used to bring happiness to people who need the aid of a special animal, a warm paw, and a friendly, furry face. Therapy dogs are used in nursing homes, hospitals, schools, and for special needs groups. The people who train dogs for therapy are generally volunteers who perform this duty as a public service. The dogs require basic obedience training prior to becoming certified as therapy dogs.

For more information see:
www.therapydogs.com
www.tdi-dog.org
www.deltasociety.org/home.htm

Dog Carting, Sledding, Drafting, Weight Pulling

This section is for dogs that are involved in the sport of pulling. Each category has its own set of criteria, but the one factor that they have in common is conditioning. These dogs are athletes and cannot be couch potatoes in order to do this work.

Weight Pulling

These dogs compete in their own weight categories and are graded on the percentage of their own body weight that they can pull. Dogs have to be able to pull an empty sled to begin with but then may pull up to ten times their body weight.

For more information see the following sites:
www.dogscouts.com/weightpull.shtml
www.iwpa.net
International Weight Pulling Society
www.adba.cc/
American Dog Breeders Association

Sled Pulling

Dog sledding is a popular sport in snow country. Dogs of choice are the Nordic types such as Siberian Huskies, Alaskan Malamutes, and Samoyeds. These dogs are born with the instinctive desire to pull.

For further information see the following sites:
www.isdra.corg

International Sled Dog Racing Association
www.dogsledding.com
www.sdas.org.uk/sledding.htm
Sled Dog Association of Scotland

Carting & Drafting

Carting is a popular sport with the Mastiff breeds. Carting (aka drafting) uses the dog's strength and endurance to pull supplies and sometimes even the family's children in carts.

For more information see the following sites:

www.cartingwithyourdog.com
For information of equipment and clubs
www.mastiff25.tripod.com/carting/
Explains carting for Mastiffs

Dog Games: Dock Diving, Flyball, Frisbee

The following games allow dogs and owners to play together and have a good time while competing with others. Although these are games, they are highly competitive and require a good deal of training and conditioning to make the handler and dog competitive.

Dock Diving

Dog diving is fun for both the competitors and fans alike. The dock diving competition is a sport where dogs chase a bumper off of a dock (or a swimming pool that allows for long distance jumping) to see how far the dog can reach before hitting the water. This is a broad jump into water and is fun for all.

For more information see the following sites:
www.dockdogs.com
www.dogplay.com/activities/dockdiving.html

Frisbee Competitions

Frisbee competitions are fun for dogs, handlers, and audiences. These competitions have evolved over the years into spectacles that are even seen at half time events at national sports competitions. Routines are choreographed to music and can involve the dogs weaving through the owners legs and leaping off of their backs to catch the Frisbee.

For more information please see the following sites:
www.iddha.com
International Disc Dog Handlers Association
www.k9frisbee.com

A web site that gives you information on upcoming events and links to various clubs

Flyball

Flyball is a relay race that involves a team of dogs and handlers. It is a fast action race that is fun for handlers, dogs, and the audience. The dogs must race over jumps, then hit a box which pops a ball into the mouth of the dog. Then the dog must race back over the jumps with the ball in his mouth before the next dog can go. The team that completes the race successfully in the fastest time wins.

For more information see the following sites:
www.flyball.com
Gives you information on teams in your area
www.flyball.org
North American Flyball Association

ABOUT THE AUTHOR

George and Karen Duet are the owners of Kingsden's Kennels, K-9 Companions Dog Training, and K-9 Security & Detection Int'l LLC.

Kingsden's Kennels has been breeding top quality dogs since 1979, among them Rottweilers, German Shepherds, Belgian Malinois, Bouvier des Flandres, and Boerboels (South African Mastiffs). Dogs under the Kingsden's name have been successfully shown to breed Championships, Schutzhund and French Ring titles, as well as obedience and agility titles, among others.

K-9 Companions Dog Training has been serving the Southwestern United States since 1979. K-9 Companions specializes in Problem Solving, Obedience, Home Manners, and Management. In addition, they train qualified dogs and handlers in advanced obedience, agilities, and service dog training.

K-9 Security & Detection Int'l LLC is also a Trademark of K-9 Companions. This division is directed towards the use of K-9's for security purposes. Dogs are trained for home and family protection, business protection, personal protection, and executive and VIP security using handler dog teams. Dogs in this division are trained in security, patrol, and explosives detection, and police K-9 training, determined by the needs of the client. The Duets are certified Personal Protection Specialists (PPS), a title bestowed upon them by The Executive Protection Institute, Berryville, Virginia. They have pioneered and taught The Use of K-9's in Executive Protection around the country to individuals involved in Police, Military, and Security. In 2000, they were presented with a Lifetime Achievement Award from Nine Lives Associates, an internationally recognized security association of protection agents who specialize in dignitary and celebrity protection. George Duet is retired from the U.S. Army after serving 20 years working in Special Operations, protecting the freedoms of his country.

Other titles they have authored are: *The Home & Family Protection Dog*, Howell Book House, 1993 By Karen Freeman Duet & George Duet; *The Business Security K-9*, Howell Book House, 1995 By Karen Freeman Duet & George Duet; and *Advanced Schutzhund*, Howell Book House, 1999 By Ivan Balabanov & Karen Duet. This last title was nominated for a Maxwell Award for excellence in the Dog Training category.

To contact the Duets:

Kingsden's K-9 Companions-K-9 Security & Detection Int'l LLC

www.K-9Companions.com

K9CoK9Sec@aol.com

1-800-870-5926 (toll free)

951-780-5810 (local)

951-780-2128 (fax)

The addition of a well trained, well mannered, and well socialized dog can be the stuff that family memories are made of.

A LETTER FROM THE AUTHOR

Sometimes it is easier for us to understand a subject we are not familiar with by associating certain aspects of the new subject with things with which we are more familiar. This is what we have attempted to do in this book. Since most people in the United States are familiar with our school system and the various levels of development that accompany the various stages of children's lives, we have attempted to draw those parallels for you here.

If your desires for your dog only go as far as enjoying him as a family pet in and around the house, you may need nothing more than an elementary school education. If you wish to be able to take him out in public and on vacations with you, a middle school or high school education may be more appropriate.

If, however, you wish to attain a title or certification, you will need a High School education as a prerequisite to your college degree, and you will need to choose an area of expertise that is suitable to your dog, just as you would choose a Major in college. It is our hope that in organizing this book in such a way, we have made your choices more clear and your path easier to discern. Whatever you do, we hope that you enjoy the process of getting there, and that the process itself creates a greater bond between you and your K-9 Companion.

Sincerely,
George and Karen Duet
K-9 Companions Dog Training
www.K-9Companions.com

GLOSSARY OF TERMS

AD title The endurance degree in Schutzhund. The dog must trot beside his handler's bicycle for 12 miles. He must have sufficient stamina to do this in the allotted amount of time and then complete a few simple obedience exercises.

AKC American Kennel Club The largest and most recognized dog registry in the United States.

AKC Titles Titles bestowed upon registered dogs by the American Kennel Club in various events. Titles are as follows: Information provided by AKC.Org (titles).

AJP Excellent Agility Jumpers With Weavers "A" Preferred.
For a title dog must earn 3 qualifying scores in Excellent "A" Jumpers With Weavers Preferred class under at least 2 different judges.

AX Agility Excellent. The dog must earn 3 qualifying scores in Excellent "A" agility class under at least 2 different judges.

AXJ Excellent Agility Jumper. The dog must earn 3 qualifying scores in Excellent A Jumpers with Weavers class under 2 different judges.

AXP Agility Excellent A Preferred. The dog must earn 3 qualifying scores in Agility Excellent "A" Preferred Class under at least 2 different judges.

CD Companion Dog. The letters CD may be added at the end of the dogs name when it has been certified under 3 different judges to have received qualifying scores in Novice Obedience Classes at three licensed trials.

CDX Companion Dog. Excellent The letters CDX may be added after the name of the dog when it has been certified by 3 different judges to have received qualifying scores Open Obedience Classes at 3 licensed trials.

HI Herding Intermediate. The dog must have 3 qualifying scores in the intermediate classes from 3 different judges at 3 different trials.

HIAdsc Herding Intermediate. Course A. (ducks, sheep, cattle) The dog must receive 3 qualifying scores in the Intermediate Course A classes using ducks, sheep, or cattle from 3 different judges at 3 different trials.

HIBdsc Herding Intermediate Course B. (ducks, sheep, cattle) The dog must receive 3 qualifying scores in the intermediate course B classes using ducks, sheep, or cattle from 3 different judges at 3 different trials.

HICs Herding Intermediate Course C. (sheep) The dog needs 3 qualifying scores from 3 different judges at 3 different trials.

HS Herding Started The dog needs 3 qualifying scores in the Started Class under 3 different judges at 3 different trials.

HSAdsc Herding Started Course A (ducks, sheep, cattle) The dog needs 3 qualifying scores in the Started "A" Class using ducks, sheep, or cattle.

HSBdsc Herding Started Course B (ducks, sheep, cattle) The dog needs 3 qualifying scores in the Started Class B from 3 different judges at 3 different trials.

HT Herding Tested: For a title, a dog must qualify twice under 2 different judges. Dog may qualify twice in one day at the same event provided it is judged under 2 different judges.

HX Herding Excellent: Three qualifying scores in the Advanced Classes from 3 different judges at 3 different trials.

HXAdsc Herding Advanced Score A (ducks, sheep, cattle): Three qualifying scores under 3 different judges, at 3 different trials, in the Advanced Class A.

HXBdsc Herding Advanced Course C (sheep): Three qualifying scores, from 3 different judges, at 3 different trials, in the Advanced B classes, using ducks, sheep, or cattle.

HXCs Herding Advanced Course (sheep): Three qualifying scores in Advance Course C classes using sheep (HIAs) from 3 different judges at 3 different trials.

JC Junior Courser: A hound running alone shall receive certification from a Judge on one date, and a second certification from a different Judge at a later date, stating that the hound completed a 600-yard course with a minimum of four (4) turns. The hound must complete the course with enthusiasm and without interruption. The **two runs can be on the same date at or in conjunction with a National Breed Specialty.**

JE Junior Earthdog: A dog must have a record of having qualified in the Junior Earthdog test in two (2) AKC licensed or member club tests under two different Judges.

JH Junior Hunter:

For a title, dog must receive qualifying scores at 4 licensed or member tests.

LCX Lure Courser Excellent: Any dog that has been awarded the title of Field Champion and has earned

45 additional championship points will be awarded the suffix title of Lure Courser Excellent (LCX). The title of Lure Courser Excellent is a cumulative title; each time the dog accrues an additional 45 championship points, it would be eligible to receive the next title level. (LCX II, LCX III, LCX IV, etc.)

MC Master Courser: The Master Courser title will be awarded to hounds that have acquired the Senior Courser title and that have earned an additional twenty-five (25) qualifying scores (with competition) in either the Open, Open Veteran or Specials stake at AKC licensed or member club lure coursing trials.

ME Master Earthdog: A dog must have a record of having qualified in the Master Earthdog test at four (4) AKC licensed or member club hunting tests under two different Judges.

MFP Master Excellent FAST Preferred.

MH Master Hunter: For a title, a dog must receive qualifying scores at 6 licensed or member tests. If the dog has already received a SH, the dog need only qualify 5 times. German Wirehaired Pointers must pass a Water Test at a licensed or member field trial or hunting test held by a Specialty Club for German Wirehaired Pointers or Weimaraners.

MJP Master Excellent Jumpers With Weaves "B" Preferred:

For a title, dog must earn 10 qualifying scores in Excellent B Jumpers With Weaves Preferred Agility class under at least 2 different judges. Trial at which AX was earned does not count toward the 10.

MX Master Agility Excellent: For a title, dog must earn 10 qualifying scores in Excellent B Agility class under at least 2 different judges. Trial at which AX was earned does not count toward the 10.

MXF Master Excellent FAST.

MXJ Master Excellent Jumpers With Weaves: For a title, dog must earn 10 qualifying scores in Excellent B Jumpers With Weaves Agility class under at least 2 different judges. Trial at which AX was earned does not count toward the 10.

MXP Master Agility Excellent "B" Preferred: For a title, dog must earn 10 qualifying scores in Excellent Agility Preferred "B" class under at least 2 different judges. Trial at which AXP was earned does not count toward the 10.

NA Novice Agility: For a title, dog must earn 3 qualifying scores in Novice A and/or B Agility class under at least 2 different judges.

NAJ Novice Agility Jumper: For a title, dog must earn 3 qualifying scores in Novice A and/or B Jumpers With Weaves class under at least 2 different judges.

NAP Novice Agility Preferred: For a title, dog must earn 3 qualifying scores in Novice Agility Preferred A and/or B Agility class under at least 2 different judges.

NF Novice FAST.

NFP Novice FAST Preferred.

NJP Novice Jumpers With Weaves Preferred: For a title, dog must earn 3 qualifying scores in Novice A and/or B Jumpers With Weaves Preferred class under at least 2 different judges.

OA Open Agility: For a title, dog must earn 3 qualifying scores in Open Agility class under at least 2 different judges.

OAJ Open Agility Jumper: For a title, dog must earn 3 qualifying scores in Open Jumpers With Weaves class under at least 2 different judges.

OAP Open Agility Preferred: For a title, dog must earn 3 qualifying scores in Open Agility Preferred class under at least 2 different judges.

OF Open FAST.

OFP Open FAST Preferred.

OJP Open Jumpers With Weaves Preferred: For a title, dog must earn three qualifying scores in Open Jumpers With Weaves Preferred class under at least two different judges.

PAX Preferred Agility Excellent.

PT Pre-Trial Tested: The American Kennel Club will issue a Pre-Trial Tested certificate to an eligible dog and will permit the use of the letters PT after the name of a dog that has been certified by two different Judges to have qualified by passing two licensed or member club Pre-Trial tests. Dog may qualify twice in one day at the same event provided he/she is judged by different judges.

RN AKC Rally® Novice: The letters RN may be added after a dog's name when it has been certified by two different judges to have received qualifying scores in Novice classes at three licensed or member rally trials.

RA AKC Rally® Advanced: The letters RA may be added after a dog's name when it has been certified by two different judges to have received qualifying scores in Advanced classes at three licensed or member rally trials.

RE AKC Rally® Excellent: The letters RE may be added after a dog's name when it has been certified by two different judges to have received qualifying scores in Excellent classes at three licensed or member rally trials.

RAE AKC Rally® Advanced Excellent: To earn an RAE title, the dog must have earned qualifying scores in both Advanced B and Excellent B classes at 10 separate licensed or member rally trials. A numeric designation will indicate the number of times the dog has met the RAE requirements, i.e. RAE2, RAE3, etc.

SC Senior Courser: 1) Must be eligible to enter the open stake. That requires the dog to have obtained at least one of the following: AKC Junior Courser title or American Kennel Club Field Champion title. 2) The hound must run with at least one other hound. 3) Must receive qualifying scores at four. 4) AKC-licensed or member trials, under two different Judges or judging panels.

SE Senior Earthdog: A dog must have a record of having qualified in the Senior Earthdog test at three (3) AKC licensed or member club tests under two different Judges.

SH Senior Hunter: For a title, a dog must receive qualifying scores at 5 licensed or member tests. If the dog has already received a JH, the dog need only qualify 4 times. German Wirehaired Pointers must pass a Water

Test at a licensed or member field trial or hunting test held by a Specialty Club for German Wirehaired Pointers or Weimaraners.

TD Tracking Dog: Dog has been certified by two judges to have passed a licensed or member club TD test or at a combined TD/TDX test, or at a combined TD/VST test or a TD/TDX/VST test.

TDX Tracking Dog Excellent: Dog has been certified by two judges to have passed a licensed or member club TDX test or at a combined TDX/VST test, or a combined TD/TDX test or a combined TD/TDX/VST test.

UD Utility Dog: The American Kennel Club will issue a Utility Dog certificate for each registered dog, that has been certified by three obedience trial judges as having received qualifying Utility scores at three licensed or member obedience trials.

UDX Utility Dog Excellent: To earn a Utility Dog Excellent title, the dog must have received qualifying scores in both Open B and Utility B at 10 separate licensed or member obedience trials. The letters UDX will be followed by a numeric designation, indicating the number of times a dog has met the requirements of the UDX title as defined in the Regulations. (UDX2 for 20 qualifying scores, UDX3 for 30 qualifying scores, UDX4 for 40 qualifying scores, etc.)

VCD1 Versatile Companion Dog 1: Must complete CD, NA, NAJ, TD or CD, NAP, NJP, TD

VCD2 Versatile Companion Dog 2: Must complete CDX, OA, OAJ, TD or CDX, OAP, OJP, TD

VCD3 Versatile Companion Dog 3: Must Complete UD, AX, AXJ, TDX or UD, AXP, AJP, TDX

VCD4 Versatile Companion Dog 4: Must complete UDX, MX, MXJ, VST or UDX, MXP, MJP, VST

VST Variable Surface Tracking: Dog has been certified by both judges to have passed a licensed or member club Variable Surface Tracking test or at a combined TD/VST test or at a combined TDX/VST test or at a combined TD/TDX/VST test.

XF Excellent FAST.

XFP Excellent FAST Preferred

The following are titles that are listed in FRONT of the dog's name. These titles are bestowed by the AKC and the following was provided using their web site AKC.Org.

AFC Amateur Field Trial Champion: Earning the AFC title.

Ch. Champion: Dogs must acquire 15 points, including 2 majors won under different judges and at least one point under a third different judge. This title is for breed conformation.

CCH Bench Show Champion: Dogs must have a total of a 100 pts under two different judges and 1 Best In Show win with competition.

CT Champion Tracker: Dog must hold all 3 tracking titles (TD, TDX and VST).

DC Dual Champion: Any dog that has been awarded the title of Champion of Record (Ch.) may be designated as a "Dual Champion," after it has also been awarded the title of Field Champion (FC) or Herding Champion (HC).

FC Field Champion: Earning the FC title.

GDSC Gun Dog Stake Champion: Win 1st place in a stake that has been designated an Open Gun Dog Championship stake.

CGC Grand Champion: A Bench Show Champion must win 3 Champion Classes with competition (against all Champions).

CGF Grand Field Champion: Field Champion must win three (3) First Lines and/or First Trees in three (3) Final Lines or Final Trees at three (3) different trials with competition. At least one of the three wins must include both Final Line and Final Tree in the same trial on the same date with competition.

CSG Supreme Grand Champion: A Bench Show Champion must win 3 Champion Classes with competition. (against all Champions).

CSGF Supreme Grand Field Champion: Field Champion must win three (3) First Lines and/or First Trees in three (3) Final Lines or Final Trees at three (3) different trials with competition. At least one of the three wins must include both Final Line and Final Tree in the same trial on the same date with competition.

CGN Grand Nite Champion: Nite Champion dogs must win five casts with plus points. CGW Grand Water Race Champion: A Water Race Champion must win three (3) First Lines and/or First Trees in three (3) Final Lines or Final Trees at three different Water Races with competition. At least one of the three wins must include both Final Line and Final Tree in the same event on the same date with competition. If a hound wins both First Line and First Tree in the Final Line or Final Tree in the same race, this only counts as one win towards a Grand Water Race Champion title.

CSGW Supreme Grand Water Race Champion: A Water Race Champion must win three (3) First Lines and/or First Trees in three (3) Final Lines or Final Trees at three different Water Races with competition. At least one of the three wins must include both Final Line and Final Tree in the same event on the same date with competition. If a hound wins both First Line and First

Tree in the Final Line or Final Tree in the same race, this only counts as one win towards a Grand Water Race Champion title.

MACH Master Agility Champion: In order to acquire the title, a dog must achieve a minimum of 750 championship points and 20 double qualifying scores obtained from the Excellent B Standard Agility class and the Excellent B Jumpers With Weaves class.

HC Herding Champion: For a title, dog must receive 15 points with at least two 1sts carrying championship points, 1 of which must be for 3 pts. or better.

NAFC National Amateur Field Champion: Win 1st place in a stake that has been designated a National Amateur Championship stake.

CNC Nite Champion: Registered dogs must win five casts with plus points.

NFC National Field Champion: Win 1st place in a stake that has been designated a National Open Championship stake.

NAGDC National Amateur Gundog Champion: National Amateur Gundog Champion title is for the dog that wins 1st place in a national amateur gun dog stake at a national championship field trial event for pointing breeds.

NGDC National Gundog Champion: Win 1st place in a stake that has been designated a National Open Gun Dog Championship stake.

NOC National Obedience Champion: The winner of the annual National Obedience Invitational shall be entitled to the designation National Obedience Champion of the (year).

NOGDC National Open Gun Dog Champion: Win 1st place in a stake that has been designated a National Open Gun Dog Championship stake.

OTCH Obedience Trial Champion: Dog must have won 100 points; dog must receive at least one first place Open B, one first place Utility and a third first place ribbon in either class First places must be awarded by three different judges. Must be at all-breed events. One of the required first places may have been won at a Specialty Show. Open B must have six in competition Utility must have 3 in competition.

RGDSC Retrieving Gun Dog Stake Champion: Win 1st place in a stake that has been designated a Retrieving Gun Dog Championship stake.

CSG Supreme Grand Champion: A dog that has been designated a Grand Bench Show Champion must win three Champion Classes with competition.

CSGF Supreme Grand Field Champion: A Grand Field Champion must win three (3) First Lines and/or First Trees in three (3) Final Lines or Final Trees at three (3) different trials with competition. At least one of the three wins must include both Final Line and Final Tree in the same trial on the same date with competition.

CSGW Supreme Grand Water Race Champion: A Grand Water Race Champion must win three First Lines and/or First Trees in three Final Lines or Final Trees at three different Water Races with competition. At least one of the three wins must include both Final Line and Final Tree in the same event on the same date with competition. If a hound wins both First Line and First Tree in the Final Line and Final Tree at the same race, this only counts as one win towards a Senior Grand Race Champion title.

CSGN Supreme Grand Nite Champion: Grand Nite Champion dogs must win five casts with plus points.

TC Triple Champion: Any dog that has been awarded the title of Dual Champion (DC) and the title of Obedience Trial Champion (OTCH) or Tracking Champion (CT) or Agility Champion (MACH) may be designated as a Triple Champion.

VCCH Versatile Companion Champion: Effective January 1, 2001, title will precede the name of the dog that completes an OTCH, MACH and CT.

CWC Water Race Champion: A dog must win one First Line and one First Tree in Finals at least once on the same date and in the same Water Race with competition and have a total of 200 Championship points.

WNC World Nite Champion: Dog must win the final cast of the annual World Hunt & Show.

CWSG World Show Champion Grand Champion Dog must win first place in CHBS. Best Overall with points for dogs defeated at the annual World Hunt & Show.

ARBA American Rare Breed Association. A breed registry for dogs from around the world that may not be registered or recognized by one or more of the other national breed registries.

Article The term used to describe a hand-sized personal object, such as a wallet, neutral in color, that is dropped on the track during a test after being handled by the track layer.

Bark and Hold The exercise in the protection phase of Schutzhund where the dog runs up to the helper in the blind and stands off the helper by barking at him in close proximity. The helper remains still.

Blind The structure (permanent or portable) that conceals the helper from the dog during protection, or which the handler may hide behind during an obedience exercise where the handler is to be out of sight of the dog.

Corrections The negative inducement given to the dog to suppress an inappropriate response. A correction should never be applied to a dog that does not understand a command or is slow in learning.

Courage The willingness of the dog to subjugate his own personal safety in order to protect himself or his handler. Courage and fighting instinct are more than the dog being fearless. The dog must be willing to fight when threatened, even when the option to escape is present. In competition, the dog is awarded the rating of Pronounced, Sufficient, or Non Sufficient.

Deep Nose A desirable way of tracking where the dog takes a full scent and tracks with his nose close to the ground.

Disposition The total characteristics of the dog's ability to perform what, according to his breed standard, he is intended to do.

Dumbell An object with a cylinder in the center and two end pieces that is retrieved by the dog.

DVG (Duetcher Verband de Gebrauchshundsportvereine) German Alliance for the utility dog sports.

FH (Fahrtenhurd) The most advanced tracking title awarded by the SV. The dog must follow a stranger's track approximately 1.300 paces long, and a minimum of three hours old. The track has four articles and is intersected by cross-tracks, laid by another stranger.

Hardness The dog's capacity to ignore unpleasant experiences during protection exercises, while demonstrating maximum courage and fighting spirit.

Hard Sleeve A protective garment worn around the arm of an agitator. The hard sleeve is designed to protect the helper from injury when working a dog with a hard bite.

Heel Command in which the dog walks at the handler's left side with his shoulder in line with the handler's knee. The dog should not forge ahead or lag behind. The Dog should automatically sit whenever the handler stops.

Helper Also called agitator or decoy, this is the person used to sharpen or mold the dog's aggression. The helper is also used to stimulate aggression and teach the dog how to bite during the protection of the training.

High Nose A characteristic in tracking where the dog tracks with his nose too high off the ground. A dog with a high nose is using air scent as well as track scent.

Intelligence The dog's ability to retain what he has learned and to profit from experience. This is an important trait in a working dog.

Long Line A leash, approximately 30 feet in length, used in several phases of working dog training to condition the dog to work at a distance from the handler.

Motivation The system of inducements given to promote desired behaviors. Praise, affection, food, and toy motivation.

OFA (Orthopedic Foundation for Animals) A medical organization that rates a dog's hips as excellent, good, or fair. When a dog receives an OFA number, he is Certified to be free of hip dysplasia. An OFA number can only be issued after the dog is two years of age. The OFA also certifies elbows and many other conditions.

Schutzhund A dog sport originating in Germany that is designed to evaluate the dog's abilities in tracking, obedience, and protection. The word means "Protection Dog" in German. Schutzhund titles:

BH – Obedience Level in Schutzhund that must be obtained prior to levels that involve protection.

Sch. A Schutzhund 1 title with obedience and protection at the levels of a Schutzhund 1 but lacking the tracking elements.

Sch. 1 First level of Schutzhund with foundational tracking, obedience, and protection exercises.

Sch. 2 Second level of Schutzhund with more advanced tracking, obedience, and protection tasks.

Sch. 3 Most advanced level of Schutzhund combining tracking, obedience, and protection.

Sharpness When the threshold for sensation in a dog is low, he will overreact to stimuli. This is also known as weak nerves and is not a desirable characteristic in a working dog. The dog may be overly willing to engage in protection and may be a fear biter (sharp shy).

Shyness Generalized avoidance behavior that causes the dog to attempt to escape from a situation.

Sleeve The protective covering over the arm of the helper during the protection phase.

Spirit The zest and enthusiasm the dog shows for the work. A very desirable trait in a working dog.

Stick A flexible, lightweight weapon used to evaluate the dog's ability to withstand a threat. A stick is not meant to inflict injury.

Suit (Protection) A full body bite suit used in working dog sports such as French, Belgian, Mondio Ring, and KNPV (Netherlands Police) trials.

Tracking Scent The scent left by a person, animal or object on the ground.

Trailing A dog's habit of crossing back and forth over the track.

Training Collar A collar that slips around the dog's neck, tightening with a correction and then loosening.

UKC (United Kennel Club) Established in 1898 the UKC us tge kargest akk-breed performance-dog registry in the world. Registering dogs from all 50 states and around the world. (Taken from UKCdogs.com website)

Agility
UAGI	United Agility I
UAGII	United Agility II
UAGII	United Agility III
UAGCH	United Agility Grand Champion
UAGCHX	United Agility Champion Excellent
UGRAGCH	United Grand Agility Champion

Conformation
Ch	Champion
GRCH	Grand Champion
NGCH	National Grand Champion
NBOB	National Best of Breed

Dog Sport
FO	Family Obedience

AOB	Alert Obedience
PA	ProtectionAlert
OBl	Protection l Obedience
Pl	Protection l
OB2	Protection 2 Obedience
P2	Protection 2
PDl	Police Dog l

Obedience

UCD	United Companion Dog
UCDX	United Companion Dog Excellent
UDD	United Utility Dog
VOCH	United Obedience Champion
GOCH	United Grand Obedience Champion

Terrier Racing

UR	United Flat Racer
USR	United Steeplechaser Racer
URCH	United Flat Race Champion
USRCH	United Steeplechase Champion

Weight Pull

UWP	United Weight Puller
UWPCH	United Weight Pull Champion

UWPCHX United Weight Pull Champion Excellent
UWPCHV United Weight Pull Champion Versatile
UWPCHO United Weight Pull Champion Outstanding
UWPCHS United Weight Pull Champion Supreme

USA United Schutzhund Clubs of America The largest Schutzhund organization in America. It follows SV rules and regulations.

Viciousness Unjustified aggression, biting without provocation.

Wall Jump The scaling or climbing jump that is part of Schutzhund II and III routines.

Willingness The dog's positive reaction to his handler's commands. The dog is enthusiastic and cheerful, even without reward.

SUGGESTED READING

Abrantes, Roger. Dog Language: An Encyclopedia of Canine Behavior. Naperville, IL: Wakan Tanka Publishers 1996.

American Rescue Dog Association. Search and Rescue Dogs: Training the K-9Hero, Second Addition 2002.

Bailey, Willard. Remembering to Breathe: Inside Dog Obedience Competition, 2003.

Balabanov, Ivan and Karen Duet. Advanced Schutzhund. New York: HowellBook House 1999.

Barwig, Susan and Stewart Hillard. Schutzhund Theory and Training Methods. New York: Howell Book House 1991.

Beaman, Arthur S. Lure Coursing: Field Trailing for Sighthounds and How To Take Part, 1993.

Beauchamp, Richard G. The Simple Guide to Showing Your Dog, 2003.

Bonham, Margaret H. The Simple Guide to Getting Active With Your Dog, 2002.

Bristow-Noble, J. C. Working Terriers:Their Management, Training, and Work, Etc. (History of Hunting Series), 2005.

Burch, Mary, and Jon Bailey. How Dogs Learn, New York: Howell Book House 1999.

Campbell, William E. Behavior Problems in Dogs, 3rd Addition. Grants Pass, Oregon 1999.

Crawford, Jaquiline J, Karen Pomerinke, and Donald Smith. Therapy Pets: The Animal-Human Healing Partnership, 2003.

Davis, Kathy Diamond. Therapy Dogs: Training Your Dog to Help Others, 2002.

Duet, Karen Freeman, and George Duet. The Home and Family Protection Dog. New York: Howell Book House, 1993.

Duet, Karen Freeman and George Duet. The Business Security K-9. New York: Howell Book House, 1995.

Fogle, Bruce and Anne B. Wilson. The Dog's Mind: Understanding Your Dog's Behavior, 1992.

Fraser, Jacqueline, and Amy Ammen. Dual Ring Dog: Successful Training for Both Conformation and Obedience Competition. New York: Howell Book House, 1991.

Holland, Vergil S. and Walt Jagger. Herding Dogs: Progressive Training, 1994.

Johnson, Chuck and Blanche. Training the Versatile Hunting Dog, 2006.

Johnson, Glen R. Tracking Dog: Theory & Methods, 2003.

Lorenz, Konrad On Aggression, New York: Fine Communications, 1997.

Mueller, Betty A. About Track Laying: Guidelines for Dog Tracking Enthusiasts, 2001.

O'Conor, Pierce Terriers for Sport (History of Hunting Series- Terrier Earth Dogs) 2005.

Quinn, Tom. The Working Retrievers: The Classic Book for the Training, Care, and Handling of Retrievers for Hunting and Field Trials, 2003.

Rebmann, Andrew, and Edward David. Cadaver Dog Handbook: Forensic Training and Tactics for the Recovery of Human Remains, 2000.

Reid, Pamela. Excel-Erated Learning: Explaining How Dogs Learn and How Best to Teach Them. Oakland, CA: James and Kenneth Publishing, 1996.

Rowell, Victor. Weight Pulling for Dogs, 1989.

Sanders, William R. Enthusiastic Tracking, The Step-by-Step Training Manual, 1998.

Schubert, Hiltmar, and Andrey Kuznetsov. Detection of Explosives and Landmines (Nato Science Series II: Mathematics, Physics and Chemistry), 2002.

Schultz, Jeff. Dogs of the Iditorod, 2003.

Schutzhund USA Rule Book, United Schutzhund Clubs of America, Order on line At www.germanshepherddog.com

Sierra Nevada Dog Drivers Inc. and Bella Levorsen. Mush: A beginners Manual of Sled Dog Training, 1997.

Smith, Jason. Retrievers and Pointers, at Home and in the Field (The Complete Hunter) Creative Publishing International, 2003.

Spencer, James B. Training Retrievers for the Marshes and Meadows, 1998.

Stanart, Lorna. Working as a Therapy Dog, 2005.

Zink, Christine. Jumping from A to Z: Teach Your Dog to Soar, 1996.

Made in the USA
Columbia, SC
16 June 2023

17833570R00212